MANGA
Step by Step

Publisher:
Paco Asensio

Illustrations and texts:
Ikari Studio

Introduction:
Paz Diman

Text edition:
Antonio Moreno

Translations:
Equipo de Edición, S. L.,
Barcelona

Editorial Project:
2009 © maomao publications
Via Laietana, 32 4th fl. of. 104
08003 Barcelona, Spain
Tel. : +34 93 268 80 88
Fax : +34 93 317 42 08
www.maomaopublications.com

Created and distributed in cooperation with Frechmann Kolón GmbH www.frechmann.com

ISBN: 978-84-96805-32-3   Printed in China

MANGA
Step by Step

KOLON●

Contents / Inhalt / Sommaire / Inhoud

Introduction / Einleitung / Introduction / Inleiding

In the wake of *Astro Boy*, *Mazinger Z* and, above all, *Akira*, *otaku* culture was definitively established in the West. Moreover, the huge popularity of series like *Dragon Ball*, *Sailor Moon* and *Ranma ½* strengthened the roots of a fan base that has grown constantly ever since.

But developing a deep understanding of *manga* technique involves knowing a particular narrative language and mastering its style of illustration, in which the biggest problems are the way to convey dynamic poses and a broad range of gestures and expressions.

This book is a basic tool for people starting out in the field. Taking its archetypical characters as the base, *ninjas*, robots, witches and pilots reveal the path to a truly spectacular result. From the initial blocking-in through to lighting details, via volumes, anatomies and inkings, here are some instructive explanations that will key you in to discovering the secrets of the great masters.

Après *Astro Boy*, *Mazinger Z* et, surtout, *Akira*, la culture *otaku* s'est définitivement installée en Occident. De plus, le formidable engouement pour des séries comme *Dragon Ball*, *Sailor Moon* ou *Ranma ½* a achevé d'enraciner un fanatisme qui ne cesse depuis de grandir.

Parvenir à maîtriser pleinement la technique du *manga* exige d'en connaître le langage narratif particulier et d'en dominer le style d'illustration, le plus difficile consistant en l'occurrence à transmettre les mouvements et toutes sortes de gestes et d'expressions.

Ce livre est un instrument de première nécessité pour tous ceux qui abordent ce monde. Se servant de ses archétypes, *ninjas*, robots, sorcières et pilotes, il leur ouvre la voie vers un résultat vraiment spectaculaire. Du crayonnage initial aux détails d'éclairage –en passant par le volume, l'anatomie et les teintes-, voici donc quelques commentaires didactiques qui vous amèneront à découvrir les secrets des grands maîtres.

Mit *Astro Boy*, *Mazinger Z* und vor allem *Akira* erreichte die *otaku*-Kultur im Westen einen großen Bekanntheitsgrad, und die Beliebtheit von Serien wie *Dragon Ball*, *Sailor Moon* und *Ranma ½* sorgte für die Etablierung einer seitdem kontinuierlich wachsenden Fangemeinde.

Für ein tief gehendes Verständnis *Manga*-Technik ist es unerlässlich, die narrative Sprache und den besonderen Illustrationsstil des Manga zu kennen – die größte Herausforderung liegt dabei in der zeichnerischen Darstellung dynamischer Bewegungsabläufe und einer Vielzahl an Gesten und Gesichtsausdrücken. Dieser Band vermittelt Anfängern die wichtigsten Grundkenntnisse in diesem Bereich; als Basis dienen hierbei archetypische Charaktere wie *Ninjas*, Roboter, Hexen und Piloten. Mit Anweisungen zu Formgebung, Volumen, Anatomie, Lichteinfall und Farbgebung wird dem Leser ein Werkzeug zur Verfügung gestellt, das ihn dazu befähigt, die Geheimnisse der großen Meister zu entdecken.

In het kielzog van *Astro Boy*, *Mazinger Z* en vooral *Akira* kreeg de *otaku*-cultuur definitief voet aan de grond in het Westen. Bovendien versterkte de enorme populariteit van series als *Dragon Ball*, *Sailor Moon* en *Ranma ½* de basis van een schare fans die sindsdien gestaag is gegroeid.

Maar om de mangatechniek echt te doorgronden moet je een bepaalde verteltrant en stijl van illustreren onder de knie krijgen, waarbij het gebruik van dynamische poses en van een breed scala aan gebaren en gezichtsuitdrukkingen het moeilijkst is.

Dit boek is bedoeld voor beginners. Aan de hand van de archetypische mangapersonages wijzen ninja's, robots, heksen en piloten de weg naar een spectaculair resultaat. Van de eerste ruwe schetsen tot lichtdetails, en van volume en anatomie tot het inkleuren van de tekeningen – dit boek geeft bruikbare aanwijzingen om de geheimen van de grote meesters te ontrafelen.

The Goodies
Die Guten
Les Bons
De goeden

WARRIOR PRINCESS

While girls in fantasy stories are usually portrayed as the hero's object of desire or as a victim who needs to be rescued or defended from the forces of evil, the Warrior Princess breaks these stereotypes to incarnate the heroine who must fight for herself. The armor and the sword, which she wields with authority, characterize her as a typical *manga* or *anime* warrior.

In Fantasygeschichten sind weibliche Figuren zumeist Objekt der Begierde oder Opfer, die vor bösen Mächten gerettet oder beschützt werden müssen. Die Kriegerprinzessin hingegen durchbricht diese Klischees: Sie verkörpert eine Heldin, die für sich selbst kämpfen muss, Rüstung und Schwert geben ihr Macht und Autorität und kennzeichnen sie als typische Manga- oder Anime-Kriegerin.

Tandis que, dans les récits de *Fantasy*, les personnages féminins sont généralement représentés comme un objet de désir pour le héros ou comme une victime qu'il faut à sauver ou défendre des forces du mal, la princesse guerrière brise ces stéréotypes pour incarner une héroïne qui doit se battre pour elle-même. L'armure et l'épée, qu'elle brandit avec autorité, font d'elle un guerrier typique de *Manga* ou d'*Anime*.

Meisjes zijn in fantasieverhalen meestal het voorwerp van verlangen van de held of een slachtoffer dat moet worden gered of verdedigd tegen het kwaad. De krijgster-prinses doorbreekt die stereotiepen door de heldin te belichamen die zelf moet vechten. Het harnas en het met gezag gehanteerde zwaard typeren haar als een echte manga- of anime-krijgster.

Shape_Form_Forme_Vorm

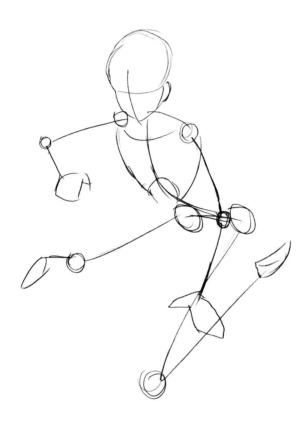

Draw a bent figure that is moving ahead while appearing to be framed in an imaginary box. Sketch her folded wings.

Zeichne eine kniende, nach vorne gebeugte Figur, die in einen imaginären Kasten eingeschlossen scheint. Deute ihre angelegten Flügel an.

Dessinez une silhouette penchée vers l'avant et comme encadrée dans une boîte imaginaire. Esquissez ses ailes repliées.

Teken een gebogen figuur die vooruit beweegt, maar gevat lijkt in een denkbeeldig kader. Schets haar ingetrokken vleugels.

Volume_Volumen_Volume_Volume

Foreshortening the back leg while tipping the wings downward achieves a sensation of depth. Match front and back perspectives.

Mehr Tiefe erreichst du, indem du das hintere Bein perspektivisch zeichnest und die Flügel nach unten verlaufen lässt. Achte auf die Übereinstimmung der Perspektiven.

Raccourcissez la partie inférieure de la jambe, tout en inclinant les ailes vers le bas, donne une sensation de profondeur. Egalisez les perspectives avant et arrière.

Door het achterste been te verkorten terwijl de vleugels naar beneden wijzen, creëer je diepte. Zorg dat het perspectief vóór klopt met achter.

Anatomy_Anatomie_Anatomie_Anatomie

Combine a beautiful body and a sweet face with an aggressive stance. Long hair flowing against the wind highlights her femininity.

Der wunderschöne Körper und das süße Gesicht werden mit einer aggressiven Körperhaltung kombiniert. Langes, im Wind flatterndes Haar betont ihre Weiblichkeit.

Combinez un beau corps et un doux visage agressive. De longs cheveux flottant au vent en rehausseront la féminité.

Combineer een prachtig lichaam en een lief gezicht met een agressieve houding. Lang haar dat in de wind golft, benadrukt de vrouwelijkheid.

Clothes_Kleidung_Vêtements_Kleren

The wings should look like something between soft metal and flesh, and the armor smoother and rounder to look more organic.

Die Flügel scheinen aus einer Kombination aus elastischem Metall und Haut zu bestehen; die Rüstung wirkt durch weiche, runde Formen organisch.

Les ailes doivent sembler à mi-chemin entre le métal souple et la chair, et, pour paraître plus naturelle, l'armure doit être aussi lisse et arrondie que possible.

De vleugels moeten eruitzien als een kruising tussen zacht metaal en vlees, maar maak het harnas gladder en ronder, meer organisch.

Lighting_Licht_Éclairage_Licht

Highlight the chrome effects by drawing irregular and fluid spots that contrast with the figure's fine, uniform contour lines.

Betone die metallischen Materialien, indem du unregelmäßige geformte Flecken einzeichnest, die mit den feinen, einheitlichen Umrisslinien der Figuren kontrastieren.

Faites ressortir les effets chromés en dessinant des taches irrégulières et fluides qui contrastent avec les contours uniformes et délicats du personnage.

Accentueer de chroomeffecten met onregelmatige, vloeiende vlekken die contrasteren met de fijne, uniforme contourlijnen van de figuur.

Color_Farben_Couleur_Kleur

Apply the color base on the clothing and hair, and then determine the other colors. Then add details requiring more definition.

Versieh Kleidung, Haare und anschließend die gesamte Figur mit den gewünschten Farben. Füge die erforderlichen Details hinzu.

Appliquez la couleur base sur les vêtements et les cheveux, puis choisissez les autres couleurs. Ensuite, ajoutez les détails qui réclament davantage de définition.

Kleur de kleren en het haar in en bepaal dan de andere kleuren. Voeg vervolgens de nodige details toe.

PRINCE

Princes are often the main characters in fantasy tales. In hundreds of stories, the prince of a forgotten kingdom becomes a hero thanks to his larger-than-life deeds. We'll use this archetype to construct our character, making him strong and attractive, while at the same time delicate and boyish.

In Fantasygeschichten übernimmt häufig ein Prinz die Hauptrolle. Hunderte von Geschichten handeln vom Prinzen eines vergessenen Königreichs, der durch seine übermenschlichen Taten zum Helden wird. Dieser Archetyp dient uns als Vorbild für unsere Figur, die stark und attraktiv, aber gleichzeitig sensibel und jungenhaft wirken soll.

Les princes sont souvent les personnages principaux des récits de *Fantasy*. Dans des centaines d'histoires, le prince d'un royaume oublié devient un héros grâce à de prodigieux exploits. Nous emploierons cet archétype pour construire notre personnage, en le faisant robuste et séduisant, mais en même temps délicat et juvénile.

Prinsen zijn vaak de hoofdfiguur in fantasieverhalen. In honderden verhalen wordt de prins van een vergeten koninkrijk een held vanwege zijn heldhaftige daden. Dit archetype dient als uitgangspunt voor ons personage, dat we sterk en aantrekkelijk, maar tegelijkertijd fijn en jongensachtig maken.

Shape_Form_Forme_Vorm

Sketch a wide arc for his arms and mark where head meets body. Draw a line from his back to his lower right leg to show movement.

Die Arme verlaufen in einem weiten Bogen. Markiere die Stelle, an der Kopf und Körper zusammentreffen. Zeichne eine Linie vom Rücken zum rechten Unterschenkel, um die Bewegung der Figur anzudeuten.

Ébauchez un arc largement ouvert pour ses bras, et marquez l'endroit où la tête rejoint le corps. Tracez une ligne depuis son dos jusqu'au bas de sa jambe droite afin de montrer le mouvement.

Teken een brede boog voor de armen en geef aan waar het hoofd en lichaam bij elkaar komen. Teken een lijn van zijn rug naar zijn rechteronderbeen om beweging te suggereren.

Volume_Volumen_Volume_Volume

Foreshorten the thorax and draw spheres for the volumes of his flexed leg and heel, and the boundary between thigh and buttocks.

Verleihe dem Brustkorb Perspektive, skizziere die Beugung von Knien und Ferse durch Kreise und markiere die Grenze zwischen Oberschenkel und Gesäß.

Raccourcissez le thorax, puis dessinez des sphères pour les volumes de la jambe en flexion et du talon, ainsi que la limite entre cuisse et fesses.

Verkort de borstkas en teken cirkels voor de volumes van zijn gebogen been en hak, en de grens tussen dij en billen.

Anatomy_Anatomie_Anatomie_Anatomie

Our prince has a slender, athletic body with well-defined muscles, but his movements should be studied and delicate.

Unser Prinz besitzt einen schlanken, athletischen Körper mit wohldefinierten Muskeln, aber seine Bewegungen sind kontrolliert und sanft.

Notre prince a un corps svelte et athlétique, avec des muscles bien définis, mais ses mouvements doivent être étudiés et délicats.

Onze prins heeft een slank, atletisch lichaam met goed gedefinieerde spieren, maar zijn bewegingen moeten bedachtzaam en fijn zijn.

Clothes_Kleidung_Vêtements_Kleren

His costume is magnificent, so choose elaborate finishes for the fabrics and armor. Jewelry and metalwork should also be ornate.

Er besitzt prächtige Kleidung, die durch sorgfältiges Zeichnen von Stoffen und Rüstung betont werden sollten. Sein Schmuck besteht aus Edelsteinen und Edelmetallen.

Son costume est grandiose, il faut donc choisir des finitions élaborées pour les tissus et l'armure. Les bijoux et la ferronnerie doivent également être ouvragés.

Het kostuum is schitterend, dus geef de stoffen en wapenrusting een fraaie afwerking. Sieraden en metaalwerk moeten ook sierlijk zijn.

Lighting_Licht_Éclairage_Licht

The shadow of his chest is projected over the rest of his body so that nearly his entire upper body is covered in shade.

Durch den Schattenwurf der Brust scheint der gesamte Oberkörper des Prinzen im Schatten zu liegen.

L'ombre du torse se projetant sur le reste du corps, la partie supérieure se trouve pratiquement ombrée.

De schaduw van de borst valt over de rest van het lichaam, zodat bijna het hele boven-lichaam beschaduwd is.

Color_Farben_Couleur_Kleur

Finish by drawing a background that complements the scene by matching the petals in the foreground. Lighten the contour lines.

Ein passender Hintergrund, aus dem die Blütenblätter in den Vordergrund zu fliegen scheinen, rundet die Szene ab. Helle die Umrisslinien auf.

Pour finir et compléter la scène, dessinez un arrière-plan assorti aux pétales du premier plan. Allégez les contours.

Rond het geheel af met een achtergrond die het tafereel aanvult door aan te sluiten bij de bloembladen op de voorgrond. Maak de contouren licht.

SD ROBOT/ IRON MAN

For the Japanese, stories about giant robots are a genre unto themselves. Stories about giant robots can take place in the future, when they serve as armored vehicles in intergalactic wars. Or they can take place in modern times, where the protagonists are usually boys who see themselves as forced to pilot giant robots in order to save humanity from some threat.

Im japanischen Kulturkreis bilden Geschichten über riesige Roboter ein eigenes Genre. Die Handlung, in der diese Roboter beispielsweise als bewaffnete Fortbewegungsmittel in intergalaktischen Kriegen dienen, kann in der Zukunft angesiedelt sein. Sie findet aber auch häufig in aktueller Zeit statt. Der Protagonist ist dann zumeist ein Junge, der einen solchen Roboter steuern muss, um die Menschheit zu retten.

Pour les Japonais, les histoires mettant en scène des robots géants sont un genre en soi. Elles peuvent se dérouler dans le futur, les robots faisant office de véhicules blindés dans des guerres intergalactiques. Elles peuvent aussi avoir pour cadre les temps modernes, les protagonistes étant alors fréquemment de jeunes garçons contraints de piloter des robots géants afin de sauver l'humanité d'une quelconque menace.

Voor Japanners vormen verhalen over reuzenrobots een genre op zich. Verhalen over reuzenrobots kunnen plaatsvinden in de toekomst, wanneer de robots dienen als gepantserde voertuigen in intergalactische oorlogen. Of ze kunnen plaatsvinden in onze tijd. Dan zijn de hoofdfiguren vaak jongens die zich genoodzaakt zien reuzenrobots te besturen om de mensheid voor een of ander gevaar te behoeden.

Shape_Form_Forme_Vorm

Draw the structure of the robot dealing with the same kind of blocks and articulation points you would use when drawing a person.

Erstelle die Grundstruktur des Roboters, indem du die gleichen Elemente und Gelenke wie für menschliche Figuren verwendest.

Tracez la structure du robot en utilisant le même genre de blocs et de points d'articulation que vous le feriez pour dessiner un personnage.

Teken de structuur van de robot met dezelfde soort blokken en gewrichtspunten die je gebruikt wanneer je een persoon tekent.

Volume_Volumen_Volume_Volume

Draw the general outlines of the robot and boy which, because they are simple figures, will resemble those of the final version.

Zeichne die Umrisslinien des Roboters und des Jungen. Da es sich um einfache Figuren handelt, ähneln sie bereits jetzt der Endversion.

Dessinez les grandes lignes du robot et du garçon ; s'agissant de simples silhouettes, ils ressembleront à ceux de la version finale.

Teken de globale contouren van de robot en jongen. Die zullen op die van de definitieve versie lijken omdat het simpele figuren zijn.

Lighting_Licht_Éclairage_Licht

Draw some continuous shading where the dark areas contrast with the reflections.

Füge an den dunkleren Partien, die mit den reflektierenden Stellen kontrastieren, Schatten hinzu.

Dessinez des ombres continues aux endroits où les plages sombres contrastent avec les reflets.

Teken doorlopende schaduw waar de donkere delen contrasteren met de weerspiegelingen.

Color_Farben_Couleur_Kleur

The metal-tone body should convey the robot's role as a friendly protector. The boy should have lighter, more innocent colors.

Der metallische Körper sollte den Roboter als freundlichen Beschützer kennzeichnen. Verwende für den Jungen hellere, „unschuldige" Farben.

Le corps aux tons métallisés doit suggérer que le robot a pour vocation de protéger l'enfant, dont les couleurs seront plus légères, plus innocentes.

De metaalachtige tint van het lichaam moet duidelijk maken dat de robot een goedaardige beschermer is. Geef de jongen lichtere, onschuldiger kleuren.

SPACE OPERA

The term 'space opera' refers to adventure stories that occur in space. They have an old-fashioned flavor because they're inspired by old science-fiction novels. In these stories, the main character is usually an antihero, a cheeky devil who acts for his own benefit. He's a fortune hunter and outlaw who seems to have come from a pirate story set in space.

Spannende Abenteuer im Weltraum sind die Themen der „Space Opera" (Weltraumoper). Ihr leicht altmodischer Touch rührt daher, dass sie von alten Science-Fiction-Romanen inspiriert ist. In diesen Geschichten ist die Hauptfigur zumeist ein Antiheld, ein respektloser Rowdy, der völlig eigennützig handelt, ein Glücksjäger und Außenseiter, der aus einer Piratengeschichte entsprungen scheint.

Le terme *space opera* est employé pour qualifier des aventures qui se déroulent dans l'espace. Elles ont un parfum un peu désuet car elles s'inspirent de vieux romans de science-fiction. Dans ces histoires, le personnage principal est d'ordinaire un anti-héros, un impertinent qui agit pour son propre compte. C'est un aventurier, un hors-la-loi qui semble sortir tout droit d'un récit de pirate ayant pour cadre l'espace.

De term ruimtesoap slaat op avonturenver-halen die plaatsvinden in de ruimte. Ze doen ouderwets aan omdat ze geïnspireerd zijn op oude sciencefictionromans. In deze verhalen is het hoofdpersonage meestal een antiheld, een brutale schavuit die op zijn eigen voordeel uit is. Het is een gelukzoeker en bandiet die weggelopen lijkt te zijn uit een piratenverhaal.

Shape_Form_Forme_Vorm

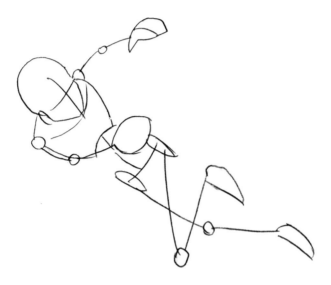

Place the figure on a curve crossing the frame. Sketch the head and trace the outline of the axis of the shoulders and hips.

Positioniere die Figur auf eine den Rahmen durchkreuzende Kurve. Skizziere den Kopf und deute die Achse zwischen Schulter und Hüften an.

Placez la silhouette le long d'une courbe en travers du cadre. Esquissez la tête et tracez le contour de l'axe des épaules et des hanches.

Plaats de figuur op een kromme lijn over de breedte van het kader. Schets het hoofd en geef de as van de schouders en heupen globaal aan.

Volume_Volumen_Volume_Volume

Begin by drawing the head, shoulders and arms since in this position they will be located in front of the pelvis and legs.

Beginne mit dem Zeichnen von Kopf, Schultern und Armen. In dieser Körperhaltung befinden sich diese Körperteile vor Beinen und Hüfte.

Commencez par dessiner la tête, les épaules et les bras ; dans cette position, ils seront situés face au bassin et aux jambes.

Teken eerst het hoofd, de schouders en de armen, want in deze positie bevinden die zich voor het bekken en de benen.

This is a slanted view of the figure, so we must foreshorten the parts nearest us and then draw the hand holding the space gun.

Die geneigte Position der Figur erfordert es, die am nächsten beim Betrachter gelegenen Körperteile perspektivisch zu gestalten und anschließend die Hand mit der Weltraumpistole hinzuzufügen.

S'agissant d'une vue en perspective, vous devez raccourcir les parties du personnage les plus proches de vous, puis dessiner la main qui tient le fusil spatial.

Omdat dit een schuin aanzicht van de figuur is, moeten we de delen die het dichtst bij ons zijn verkorten en dan de hand met het ruimtepistool tekenen.

Clothes_Kleidung_Vêtements_Kleren

Space adventurers wear tight-fitting clothes with a strap across their chest. The weapon design evokes the spirit of pulp fiction.

Weltraumhelden tragen enge Kleidung mit Brustgurt. Die Aufmachung der Waffe erinnert an Groschenromane.

Les aventuriers de l'espace portent des vêtements ajustés, avec une sangle en travers de la poitrine. Les lignes du fusil évoquent l'esprit *pulp-fiction*.

Ruimteavonturiers dragen strakke kleren en een riem. De stijl van de wapens is geïnspireerd op pulpfictie.

Lighting_Licht_Éclairage_Licht

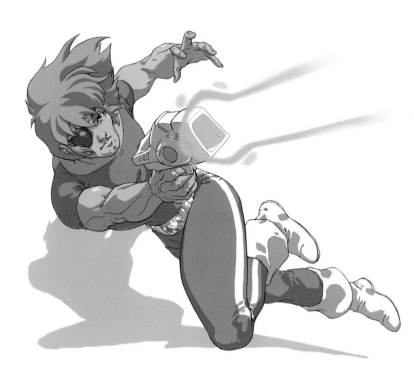

Here light comes from the gun ray. Place shiny spots on the torso and legs, and denser shadows on the shoulders, arms and head.

Die Lichtquelle ist hier der Strahl der Waffe. Gib auf Oberkörper und Beine hellere Flecken; Schultern, Arme und Kopf werden mit Schatten versehen.

Ici, la lumière vient de l'arme à laser. Placez des taches brillantes sur le torse et les bras, et des ombres plus consistantes sur les épaules, les bras et la tête.

Hier komt het licht van de straal van het pistool. Teken lichte plekjes op de romp en benen en dichtere schaduwen op de schouders, armen en het hoofd.

Color_Farben_Couleur_Kleur

Draw the deformed silhouette of the character as a gray-colored spot. Color the suit in dramatic, pulp-fiction colors.

Der seltsam geformte Schatten der Figur besteht aus einem grauen Fleck, während der Anzug grelle, dramatisch wirkende Farben erhält.

Donnez à l'ombre portée du personnage l'aspect d'une tâche grise. Teintez le reste à l'aide de couleurs vives et spectaculaires.

Teken het vervormde silhouet van het personage als een grijze vlek. Geef het pak opvallende, pulpfictieachtige kleuren.

COWBOY

Westerns make us think of rural landscapes, action-packed stories and lonely heroes surviving in a hostile world thanks to their quick draw and sharpshooting talents. We have taken some liberties by drawing an attractive young man with long hair. We can help create an Old West atmosphere with a wide-brimmed hat in the picture and the desert as a background.

Der Begriff „Western" lässt uns an weite Landschaften, actionreiche Storys und einsame Helden denken, die nur dank ihrer Reaktionsfähigkeit und Schießkünste in einer feindlichen Welt überleben. Beim Zeichnen dieses attraktiven, langhaarigen jungen Mannes haben wir völlige Freiheit. Ein breitkrempiger Hut und die Wüste im Hintergrund verliehen der Szene eine Western-Atmosphäre.

Le western évoque les grands espaces, les histoires truffées d'action et les héros solitaires qui survivent dans un monde hostile parce qu'ils dégainent vite et tirent mieux encore. Nous avons pris quelques libertés en dessinant ce séduisant jeune homme aux cheveux longs. On peut encore accentuer l'atmosphère western en le coiffant d'un chapeau à larges bords, avec un désert à l'arrière-plan.

Bij westerns denken we aan weidse landschappen, verhalen vol actie en eenzame helden die zich als razendsnelle scherpschutters staande houden in een vijandige wereld. We hebben de vrijheid genomen een aantrekkelijke jonge man met lang haar te tekenen. Met een breed gerande hoed en een woestijn als achtergrond kun je een wildwestsfeer creëren.

Shape_Form_Forme_Vorm

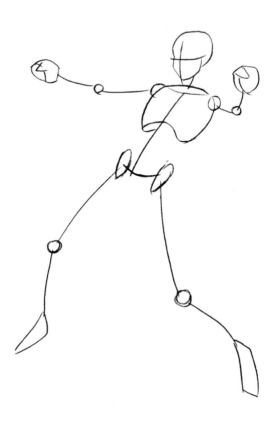

Start by arching his back backward. Then give the figure some motion by drawing him with arms and legs open but slightly bent.

Beginne mit dem nach hinten gelehnten Rücken. Gib der Figur anschließend Bewegung, indem du sie mit geöffneten, aber leicht abgewinkelten Armen und Beinen zeichnest.

Commencez par cambrer son dos vers l'arrière. Ensuite, donnez du mouvement au personnage en le dessinant jambes et bras écartés, mais légèrement penché.

Laat eerst de rug naar achteren buigen en teken vervolgens de armen en benen tamelijk gespreid en licht gebogen om de figuur beweging te geven.

Volume_Volumen_Volume_Volume

Follow the axis of the back to draw the blocks forming the chest. His foreshortened left arm and bended legs can be a bit tricky.

Folge der Rückenachse und füge die Brustpartie hinzu. Es ist nicht ganz einfach, den linken Arm und das linke Bein perspektivisch zu zeichnen.

Suivez l'axe du dos pour dessiner les blocs composant le torse. Le bras gauche raccourci et les jambes fléchies peuvent poser quelques problèmes.

Volg de as van de rug om de blokken te tekenen waaruit de borst is opgebouwd. De verkorte linkerarm en gebogen benen kunnen wat lastig zijn.

Anatomy_Anatomie_Anatomie_Anatomie

The head does not seem very convincing. Let's redraw it on a separate piece of paper and substitute it for the first version.

Der Kopf ist noch nicht gelungen. Wir zeichnen ihn auf einem anderen Blatt Papier erneut und ersetzen damit die erste Version.

La tête n'est pas très convaincante. Redessinez-la sur une feuille de papier à part, et substituez cette nouvelle version à la première.

Het hoofd ziet er niet erg overtuigend uit. Laten we op een apart vel papier een tweede versie tekenen ter vervanging van de eerste.

The jacket floats in the air forming folds that follow the movement. Correct the revolver to make it look more solid.

Die im Wind wehende Jacke bildet Falten, die der Bewegung folgen. Korrigiere den Revolver und lasse ihn solider wirken.

La veste flotte au vent, formant des plis qui suivent le mouvement. Rectifiez le revolver pour lui donner une apparence plus robuste.

De jas zweeft in de lucht en vormt plooien die de beweging volgen. Corrigeer de revolver zodat hij meer body krijgt.

Lighting_Licht_Éclairage_Licht

Draw the folds of the tattered raincoat with shadowy outlines. Also draw a shadow extending from the figure's feet.

Die Falten des zerfledderten Mantels entstehen durch Schattierungen, ebenso werfen die Beine der Figur Schatten.

Dessinez les plis de l'imperméable en lambeaux et en ombrant les contours. Dessinez aussi une ombre portée entre les pieds du personnage.

Geef de plooien van de sjofele regenjas schaduwcontouren. Teken ook een schaduw die zich uitstrekt vanaf de voeten.

ight, chamois-colored
clothes complement
the desert background.
Complete the image
with a cloud of dust
near the gunman's feet.

Die helle, lederfarbene
Kleidung passt
hervorragend zur Wüste
im Hintergrund. Eine
Staubwolke an den
Füßen des Cowboys
rundet das Bild ab.

Des vêtements de
couleur chamois clair
complètent le désert en
arrière-plan.
Parachevez l'image en
dessinant un nuage de
poussière près des
pieds du pistolero.

Lichte, zeemkleurige
kleren sluiten aan bij de
woestijnachtergrond.
Rond het geheel af met
een stofwolk aan de
voeten van de schutter.

TECHNO-PET

he techno-pet is a kind of virtual creature
hat seems to appear as a hologram or a
hape of light that suddenly takes a physical
orm. These types of stories are very
requently based on the relationship between
hildren and their pets, and they extol ethics,
alues and responsibility, as well as feelings
f friendship and comradeship in the kids.

Beim „Techno-Pet" handelt es sich um eine
Art virtuelle Kreatur, die als Hologramm oder
Lichtgebilde erscheint und ganz plötzlich
Gestalt annimmt. In solchen Geschichten
geht es häufig um die Freundschaft zwischen
Kindern und ihren Haustieren – Moral, Werte
und Verantwortung ebenso wie Freundschaft
und Kameradschaftlichkeit stehen im
Mittelpunkt.

e *techno-pet* est une sorte de créature
rtuelle se présentant sous l'apparence d'un
ologramme ou d'une forme lumineuse qui,
oudainement, prend corps. Ce genre
'histoires, très souvent basées sur l'amitié
ntre des enfants et leurs animaux familiers,
xaltent les valeurs éthiques et la
esponsabilité, ainsi que les sentiments
'amitié et de camaraderie.

De techno-pet is een soort virtueel dier dat
verschijnt als een hologram of een gestalte
van licht die plotseling een lichamelijke vorm
aanneemt. Verhalen met dit soort wezens
zijn vaak gebaseerd op de relatie tussen
kinderen en hun huisdieren en verheerlijkt
normen en waarden en verantwoordelijkheid,
evenals gevoelens van vriendschap en
kameraadschap bij de kinderen.

Shape_Form_Forme_Vorm

Before drawing the child, draw two lines that determine the position of the board.

Deute zunächst mit zwei Linien die Position des Boards an und zeichne dann das Kind darauf.

Avant de dessiner l'enfant, tracez deux lignes pour déterminer la position de la planche à roulettes.

Trek, voordat je het kind tekent, twee lijnen die de positie van het bord aangeven.

The boy's feet should be located on the plane delimited by the board. The eagle's huge wings should not overpower the body.

Die Füße des Jungen stehen genau auf der Fläche des Boards. Achte darauf, dass die riesigen Flügel des Adlers nicht übertrieben wirken.

Les pieds du garçon doivent se situer sur le plan délimité par la planche. Les larges ailes d'aigle ne doivent pas écraser le corps.

Plaats de voeten van de jongen op het vlak dat begrensd wordt door het bord. De enorme vleugels van de adelaar mogen het lichaam niet overschaduwen.

Anatomy_Anatomie_Anatomie_Anatomie

Draw each eye-catching character separately, so you can focus on their design and not on the way they overlap.

Zeichne die beiden Charaktere einzeln, so kannst du dich auf ihre Gestaltung konzentrieren und musst nicht auf die Überschneidungen achten.

Dessinez ces personnages haut en couleurs séparément, de manière à vous concentrer sur eux et non sur la façon dont ils s'imbriquent.

Teken elk markant personage apart, zoda je je kunt concentrere op hun ontwerp en nie op het overlappen van de figuren.

The strongest light comes from the boy's device but the logo that the techno-pet has round its neck also lights up.

Das Emblem des Jungen ist die stärkste Lichtquelle, das Logo am Hals des Techno-Pet leuchtet ebenfalls.

La lumière la plus forte provient de l'engin du garçon, mais le logo que le *techno-pet* porte autour du cou s'illumine également.

Het felste licht komt van het apparaat van de jongen, maar het embleem om de hals van de techno-pet geeft ook licht.

Color_Farben_Couleur_Kleur

Use flat colors for the outlines, representing volumes with flat, well-defined shadows. The sky stands out because of its realism.

Verwende Basisfarben für die Umrisslinien, um flache, wohldefinierte Schatten zu erhalten. Der Himmel sticht durch seine realistische Gestaltung besonders ins Auge.

Utilisez des couleurs primaires pour les contours, et représentez les volumes avec des ombres plates bien définies. Le ciel se caractérise par son réalisme.

Gebruik primaire kleuren voor de contouren en geef de volumes scherpe schaduwen. De lucht springt eruit vanwege zijn realistische weergave.

Finish_Fertigstellung_Finition _Afwerking

Add more effects with white trails that follow the movement of the figures, creating an extremely dynamic scene.

Mit effektvollen weißen Spuren, die den Bewegungen der Figuren folgen, erhältst du eine extrem dynamische Atmosphäre.

Accentuez les effets à l'aide de traînées blanches dans le prolongement du mouvement des personnages, créant ainsi une scène extrêmement dynamique.

Voeg nog meer effecten toe met witte sporen die de beweging van de figuren volgen, zodat er een zeer dynamisch geheel ontstaat.

STAR PILOT

This battle spaceship pilot is very self-confident, with an air of superiority, but without being arrogant. The design of his suit must be original, visually striking and attractive. However, the fighter he is piloting must be modern, light and maneuverable. To draw it we must pay close attention to proportions and employ all our knowledge about perspective.

Dieser Pilot eines Kriegs-Raumschiffs strahlt Selbstbewusstsein und Überlegenheit aus, ohne arrogant zu wirken. Sein Anzug hat ein originelles, auffälliges und attraktives Design. Beim Zeichnen seines modernen, leichten, wendigen Raumschiffs müssen wir besonders auf die Proportionen und die richtige Perspektive achten.

Très sûr de lui, ce pilote de vaisseau spatial de combat affiche un léger air de supériorité, sans arrogance toutefois. La conception de son costume doit être originale, frappante et à la fois séduisante à l'œil. Quant au vaisseau de chasse qu'il pilote, il sera moderne, léger et maniable. Pour le dessiner, vous devez accorder beaucoup de soin aux proportions et employer toutes vos connaissances en matière de perspective.

Deze piloot van een ruimteslagschip is buitengewoon zelfverzekerd en heeft een air van superioriteit, maar zonder arrogant te zijn. Het ontwerp van het pak moet origineel, opvallend en aantrekkelijk zijn. Het schip dat hij bestuurt, moet daarentegen modern, licht en wendbaar zijn. Let bij het tekenen ervan heel goed op de proporties en het perspectief.

Shape_Form_Forme_Vorm

Do a simple sketch of the ship. Draw a relaxed posture, with the legs open.

Erstelle zunächst eine einfache Skizze des Schiffs. Der Pilot steht in entspannter Haltung, mit geöffneten Beinen.

Faites une simple ébauche du vaisseau. Dessinez le personnage dans une position détendue, jambes écartées.

Maak een eenvoudige schets van het schip. Geef het personage een ontspannen pose met de benen uit elkaar.

Volume_Volumen_Volume_Volume

Slightly raise the right shoulder and the left hip. Integrate the ship behind the character.

Rechte Schulter und linke Hüfte sind leicht angehoben, das Raumschiff befindet sich hinter der Figur.

Surélevez légèrement l'épaule droite et la hanche gauche. Insérez le vaisseau derrière le personnage.

Teken de rechter-schouder en linker-heup wat hoger. Teken het schip als achtergrond van het personage.

Anatomy_Anatomie_Anatomie_Anatomie

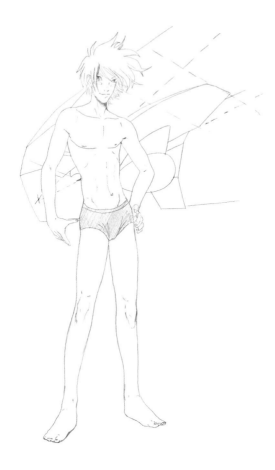

Well-developed, muscular and athletic body. The wind blows the character's hair.

Der Körper ist muskulös und athletisch, das Haar weht im Wind.

Corps athlétique, musclé et bien développé. Le vent ébouriffe la chevelure du personnage.

Het lichaam is goed ontwikkeld, gespierd en atletisch. De wind waait door het haar van de piloot.

Give detail to the external structure of the ship. Detail the pilot's uniform with insignias, protection and decorations.

Detailliere die äußere Form des Raumschiffs und die Uniform des Pilots mit Schmuck, Abzeichen und Schutzvorrichtungen.

Ornementez la structure externe du vaisseau. Agrémentez l'uniforme du pilote avec des insignes, des protections et des décorations.

Breng details aan in de buitenkant van het schip. Voorzie het uniform van de piloot van insignes, beschermende delen en onderscheidingen.

Lighting_Licht_Éclairage_Licht

Apply the shadows mainly on the character, to emphasize him instead of the ship, which will remain in the background.

Versieh vor allem die Figur mit Schatten, um diese hervorzuheben und das Raumschiff in den Hintergrund zu rücken.

Appliquez les ombres, essentiellement sur le personnage, pour le mettre en valeur plutôt que le vaisseau, qui doit rester à l'arrière-plan.

Voorzie vooral het personage van schaduw om de piloot te accentueren in plaats van het schip, dat op de achtergrond blijft.

se vivid colors for the
niform and cold tones
r the ship. The outline
colored to give
eater depth without
anding out.

Verwende lebhafte
Farben für die Uniform
und kühlere Töne für
das Raumschiff. Die
Umrisslinie ist farbig
und gibt so mehr Tiefe,
ohne hervorzustechen.

Utilisez des couleurs
vives pour l'uniforme et
des tons froids pour le
vaisseau. Les contours
sont discrètement
colorés pour accentuer
la profondeur.

Gebruik levendige
kleuren voor het
uniform en koele tinten
voor het schip. De
contouren zijn in kleur
om meer diepte te
creëren zonder eruit te
springen.

MAGICAL GIRL

Magical girls are young girls who obtain special powers as a result of magical phenomena or other similar means. The crisis point in the story is always solved with a transformation scene, in which the girl changes into her magical-girl uniform. These stories often include some type of object or special symbol in the air that serves as a catalyst of magical energy.

„Magical Girls" (magische Mädchen) sind junge Mädchen, die aufgrund magischer Phänomene o. ä. über besondere Kräfte verfügen. Der gefährlichste Moment einer Geschichte wird stets mit einer Verwandlungsszene gelöst, in der das Mädchen in seine Magical Girl-Uniform schlüpft. Häufig tauchen in diesen Geschichten Objekte oder besondere Symbole in der Luft auf, die die magische Energie verstärken.

Les magical girls sont des jeunes filles qui ont été investies de pouvoirs spéciaux à la suite d'un phénomène magique ou d'un événement analogue. Le moment critique où l'histoire se dénoue est toujours une scène de transformation où l'héroïne revêt son uniforme de magical-girl. Ces histoires mettent fréquemment en jeu un objet ou un symbole aérien spécial, qui sert à catalyser l'énergie magique.

Magische meisjes zijn jonge meisjes die speciale krachten verkrijgen door magische verschijnselen of tovermiddelen. De crisis in het verhaal wordt altijd opgelost met een transformatiescène waarin het meisje haar magische uniform aankrijgt. In deze verhalen zit vaak een object of speciaal symbool in de lucht, als een katalysator van magische energie.

Shape_Form_Forme_Vorm

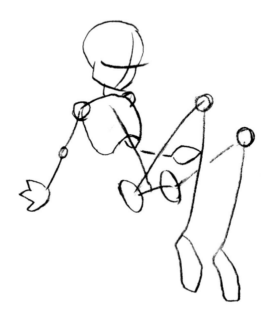

The figure is seated, leaning backward, with its arms spread apart as if on an air mattress that keeps it from falling abruptly.

Die sitzende Figur lehnt sich zurück und stützt sich mit den Armen ab, um nicht umzukippen.

En position assise, le personnage s'appuie vers l'arrière, bras écartés, comme s'il reposait sur un coussin d'air l'empêchant de chuter.

De figuur zit achterover geleund, de armen gespreid alsof ze op een luchtmatras ligt d ervoor zorgt dat ze nie plotseling valt.

ake the legs overlap
e torso and the pelvis
d the abdomen their
vn spaces while being
oportionate to the
her features.

Die Beine liegen vor
dem Oberkörper; Hüfte
und Unterkörper, die
proportional zum
restlichen Körper sein
müssen, erhalten
eigenen Raum.

Superposez jambes et
torse, mettez en place
bassin et abdomen en
veillant à respecter les
proportions.

Laat de benen de romp
overlappen en geef het
bekken en de buik hun
volumes, maar wel in
de juiste verhouding tot
de rest.

Anatomy_Anatomie_Anatomie_Anatomie

Because the figure is not complicated, drawing the anatomy is like sketching volumes.

Aufgrund der unkomplizierten Struktur der Figur gestaltet sich das Zeichnen ihrer Anatomie wie das Erstellen einer einfachen Skizze.

La figure n'étant pas compliquée, dessiner l'anatomie revient à peu près à esquisser des volumes.

Omdat de figuur niet complex is, gaat het b de anatomie min of meer slechts om volumes tekenen.

The real difficulty is the complexity of the costume. Start by drawing the costume's main volumes.

Die wahre Schwierigkeit liegt im Zeichnen ihrer Kleidung. Beginne daher zunächst mit deren Hauptelementen.

La vraie difficulté tient à la complexité du costume. Commencez par en dessiner les principaux volumes.

Wel lastig is het complexe kostuum. Begin met de ruimtelijke vorm van het kostuum.

Lighting_Licht_Éclairage_Licht

Light comes from the magical effect surrounding the girl. Spotlights shine on the figure, accentuating shadows in darker areas.

Das Licht stammt aus den magischen, das Mädchen umgebenden Effekten. Durch das Scheinwerferlicht erhalten die dunkleren Bereiche Schatten.

La lumière vient du halo magique qui entoure la jeune fille. Les projecteurs sont braqués sur le personnage, accentuant les ombres dans les zones plus sombres.

Het licht komt van het magische effect om he meisje heen. Spotlight beschijnen de figuur e accentueren schadu- wen in donkere delen.

Highlight the magical girl's uniform with the yellow in the dress, boots and wand.

Durch die Gelbtöne in Kleid, Stiefeln und Zauberstab werden besondere Akzente gesetzt.

Faites ressortir l'uniforme de la *magical girl* grâce au jaune de la robe, des bottes et du sceptre.

Accentueer het uniform van het magische meisje met het geel in de jurk, laarzen en staf.

LITTLE WITCH

hese witches combine their daily life
racticing the art of magic with the purpose
f doing good and helping others without
evealing their special abilities. When it's
me to use their powers, they dress up in
utfits inspired by the classic iconography
ut with a much more simplistic touch, and
ey always make use of objects like magic
ats and flying brooms.

Diese Hexen wenden ihre magischen Kräfte
im Alltagsleben an, um anderen durch gute
Taten zu helfen; ihre Fähigkeiten bleiben
dabei aber unentdeckt. Wenn sie den
Zeitpunkt gekommen sehen, ihre Kräfte
einzusetzen, schlüpfen sie in ihr Kostüm.
Dieses enthält klassische Elemente, ist aber
sehr einfach gestaltet und immer
ausgestattet mit Objekten wie magische
Hüte und fliegende Besen.

es sorcières concilient la vie de tous les
urs avec la pratique de la magie, pour faire
 bien et aider autrui sans révéler leurs dons
articuliers. Quand l'heure est venue d'user
e leurs pouvoirs, elles revêtent des habits
spirés de l'imagerie classique, mais en
eaucoup plus simple, et recourent toujours
des accessoires : chapeaux magiques,
alais volants.

Deze heksen combineren hun dagelijkse
toverpraktijk met het helpen van anderen
zonder dat ze daarbij hun bijzondere gaven
onthullen. Als het tijd is om hun krachten te
gebruiken, trekken ze kleren aan die
geïnspireerd zijn op de klassieke iconografie,
maar dan in een veel simpelere stijl. Verder
gebruiken ze altijd voorwerpen als
toverhoeden en vliegende bezems.

Shape_Form_Forme_Vorm

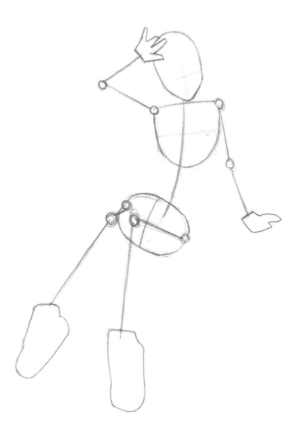

We'll begin by drawing the line of her back and hips and then we'll clearly mark the base for foreshortening her legs.

Beginne mit dem Zeichnen des Gesäßes und der Hüften, um anschließend die perspektivisch ausgerichteten Beine anzudeuten.

Nous commencerons par tracer la ligne de son dos et de ses hanches, puis nous marquerons clairement la base pour raccourcir ses jambes.

We tekenen eerst de lijn van de rug en heupen. Daarna geven we duidelijk de basis aan voor het verkorten van de benen.

We'll look for simple shapes and give her hips some nice volume considering her pose, but without forgetting that she is a child.

Zeichne die Figur aus einfachen Formen und betone ihre Hüfte, vergiss dabei aber nicht, dass sie ein Kind ist und berücksichtige ihre Körperhaltung.

Nous rechercherons des formes simples et donnerons à ses hanches de jolis volumes en fonction de l'attitude du personnage, sans oublier toutefois qu'il s'agit d'une enfant.

Houd de vormen simpel en geef de heupen van het heksje aardig wat volume in verband met haar pose, maar vergeet niet dat het een kind is.

Anatomy_Anatomie_Anatomie_Anatomie

Pay attention to how her legs hang suspended in air. Her face should display childish features and big eyes. She should transmit happiness.

Schenke dabei besonders den in der Luft hängenden Beinen Aufmerksamkeit. Ihr Gesicht sollte kindlich wirken, große Augen besitzen und Fröhlichkeit ausstrahlen.

Faites attention à la manière dont les jambes sont suspendues dans l'air. Le visage doit avoir des traits enfantins, de grands yeux et transmettre une sensation de bonheur.

De benen hangen als het ware in de lucht. Het gezicht moet kinderlijke trekken en grote ogen hebben en blijdschap uitstralen.

We'll draw the volume of her hair and clothes considering the direction they fall in and define the basic shape of her broom.

Achte beim Zeichnen ihrer Haare und Kleidung auf deren Verlaufsrichtung, und definiere die Grundform des Besens.

Nous dessinerons le volume des cheveux et des vêtements en tenant compte de la direction dans laquelle ils tombent, puis nous définirons la forme élémentaire du balai.

Let bij het tekenen van het volume van haar haar en kleren op de richting waarin deze vallen. Geef de vorm van de bezem globaal aan.

Lighting_Licht_Éclairage_Licht

A zenithal light source projects shadows on the lower parts of objects. The witch projects a shadow over the back of her dress.

Durch das von oben einfallende Licht befindet sich der Schatten an der Unterseite der Objekte, wobei die Hexe selbst einen Schatten hinter sich auf das Kleid wirft.

Une source de lumière zénithale projette des ombres au bas des objets. La sorcière projette une ombre sur le revers de sa robe.

Een licht bovenaan werpt schaduw op de onderkant van de voorwerpen. De heks werpt een schaduw op de achterkant van haar jurk.

classical color
lection helps us
entify our character.
ing dull base colors,
'll shade her skin
d outline her eyes.

Die Figur wird durch die
klassische Farbauswahl
charakterisiert. Für die
Schattierung ihrer Haut
und die Umrandung der
Augen werden
gedeckte Basisfarben
eingesetzt.

Une sélection
chromatique classique
nous aidera à
caractériser le
personnage. A l'aide de
couleurs de base
mates, nous ombrerons
sa peau et soulig0nerons
le contour de ses yeux.

Klassieke kleuren
maken dit personage
herkenbaar. Gebruik
doffe aardtinten voor
de schaduw op de huid
en de contouren van de
ogen.

Shading_Schatten_Ombres_Schaduw

Let's use geometrical patches of color for large objects such as the broom and hat, and patches of various colors for her hair.

Verwende für größere Objekte wie Besen und Hut ähnliche Farbelemente, für das Haar jedoch verschiedene Farbtöne.

Utilisez des patches géométriques de couleur pour les objets larges tels que le balai et le chapeau, et des patches de plusieurs couleurs pour les cheveux.

Gebruik geometrische kleurvlakken voor grote voorwerpen als de bezem en hoed en meerkleurige vlakken voor het haar.

'll add lighting to
e her eyes more
rsonality and
mplete the
stration with a violet-
ored magical motif.

Lichtpunkte geben den
Augen Persönlichkeit.
Runde das Bild mit
einem magischen Motiv
in Violett ab.

Nous ajouterons de la
luminosité pour donner
aux yeux davantage de
personnalité, et nous
complèterons
l'illustration avec un
motif magique de
couleur violette.

Met een beetje licht
geven we de ogen meer
persoonlijkheid, en we
ronden de tekening af
met een violetkleurig
magisch motief.

KUNG FU

The first thing that comes to mind when thinking about martial arts is the exotic esthetic, kimonos and loose silk clothing, as well as the studied postures or the fighters' weapons. Martial arts are performed with coordinated moves where fighters look like they're dancing. Such poses are often inspired by the movements of animals, such as tigers, snakes or cranes.

Kampfsportkunst assoziieren wir mit exotischer Ästhetik, Kimonos, flatternden Seidenkleidern, einer kontrollierten Körperhaltung und den Waffen der Kämpfer. Diese Sportarten werden mit koordinierten Bewegungen ausgeführt, wobei der Kampf eher wie ein Tanz wirkt. Die Bewegungen sind häufig durch die Tierwelt inspiriert, so zum Beispiel durch Tiger, Schlangen oder Kraniche.

Quand on pense aux arts martiaux, l'esthétique exotique, les kimonos et les habits en soie très amples, ainsi que les postures étudiées ou les armes de combat, s'imposent immédiatement à l'esprit. Dans ces arts, les mouvements sont coordonnés et les combattants semblent danser. Les poses sont souvent inspirées de mouvements animaux : tigres, serpents ou grues.

Bij vechtsporten denk je het eerst aan mooie, exotische kimono's, wijde zijden kleding en weloverwogen houdingen waarin de wapens worden gehouden. Vechtsporten kennen gecoördineerde bewegingen waarbij het lijkt alsof de vechters dansen. De houdingen zijn vaak gebaseerd op de bewegingen van dieren, zoals tijgers, slangen en kraanvogels.

Shape_Form_Forme_Vorm

Sketch an undulating line descending vertically from head to feet. The back and arms are reduced to a sinuous, continuous line.

Zeichne eine wellenförmige Linie, die vertikal vom Kopf bis zu den Füßen abfällt. Rücken und Arme sind auf eine kurvige, fortlaufende Linie reduziert.

Esquissez une ligne ondulée descendant verticalement de la tête aux pieds. Le dos et les bras sont réduits à une ligne sinueuse continue.

Teken een golvende lij van het hoofd omlaag naar de voeten. De ru, en armen worden teruggebracht tot een doorlopende, golvende lijn.

e position of the
ees must reflect the
ct that she is moving
e of them ahead. Our
reshortening deforms
e extremities.

Die Knieposition muss
die Vorwärtsbewegung
der Figur anzeigen. Die
Gliedmaßen erhalten
Perspektive.

La position des genoux
doit montrer que l'un
d'eux est déplacé vers
l'avant. L'effet de
rapprochement
déforme les extrémités.

Uit de positie van de
knieën moet blijken dat
ze er één naar voren
beweegt. Door het
verkorten vertekenen
we de ledematen.

Anatomy_Anatomie_Anatomie_Anatomie

To draw a natural position, we must find the axis of the shoulders and hips, drawing the spine so it bends like a spring.

Um die Position so natürlich wie möglich erscheinen zu lassen, zeichnen wir das wie eine Feder gespannte Rückgrat auf die Achse zwischen Schulter und Hüften.

Pour dessiner une position naturelle, il faut chercher l'axe des épaules et des hanches, et tracer l'épine dorsale en la faisant ployer comme un archet.

Voor een natuurlijke houding moeten we d as van de schouders heupen vinden en de ruggengraat zo tekene dat hij buigt als een springveer.

The clothing of the kung fu fighter is complex, with fabrics that intertwine and adapt to the shoulders or hang down to the waist.

Die aufwendig gestaltete Kleidung der Kung-Fu-Kämpferin besteht aus ineinander verschlungenen Tüchern, die sich um die Schultern winden oder an der Hüfte herabhängen.

L'habillement du lutteur de kung-fu est complexe, avec des étoffes qui s'entrelacent et épousent les épaules, ou pendent de la ceinture.

De kleding van de kungfuvechters is complex, met stoffen die in elkaar verstrengeld zijn en als gegoten om de schouders zitten of omlaaghangen tot het middel.

Lighting_Licht_Éclairage_Licht

To represent the texture of silk, draw typical reflections with sinuous contours, adapting them to the folds of each garment.

Betone die glänzende Struktur der Seide durch wellenförmige Reflexionen und passe diese an den Faltenwurf der einzelnen Kleidungsstücke an.

Pour représenter la texture de la soie, dessinez-en les reflets caractéristiques aux contours sinueux, en les adaptant aux plis de chaque pièce de vêtement.

Geef de textuur van de zijde weer door middel van karakteristieke reflecties met golvende contouren die je aanpast aan de plooier van elk kledingstuk.

e costume looks
ettier with a happy
lor like pink. Lastly,
place the black lines
the design motifs
th colored lines.

Mit einer leuchtenden
Farbe, beispielsweise
Pink, verleihst du der
Kleidung eine
ansprechende Note.
Ersetze zum Schluss
die schwarzen Konturen
der Stoffmuster durch
farbige Linien.

Le costume a meilleure
allure dans des tons
gais comme le rose.
Pour finir, remplacez les
lignes noires des motifs
dessinés par des lignes
de couleur.

Het kostuum ziet er
mooier uit met een
vrolijke kleur als roze.
Vervang ten slotte de
zwarte lijnen van de
ontwerpmotieven door
gekleurde lijnen.

SAMURAI

The Samurai, a kind of soldier with privileges and lands, was a noble warrior with the right to carry a sword and armor onto the battlefield and in civilian life. Samurais dedicated their lives to the discipline of wielding their *katana*. The Samurai Code emphasized duty and sacrifice, even above the Samurai's own life, and obedience to the feudal lord and Emperor.

Bei den Samurais, eine Art Soldat mit besonderen Privilegien und Landbesitz, handelte es sich um edle Krieger mit dem Recht, Schwert und Rüstung auf dem Schlachtfeld und im zivilen Leben zu tragen. Samurais widmeten ihr Leben der Kunst, mit dem Katana (Schwert) kämpfen. Pflicht und Opferbereitschaft waren die wichtigsten Grundsätze des Samurai-Kodex – dieser stand sogar über dem eigenen Leben sowie dem Gehorsam gegenüber dem Feudalherren und Herrscher.

Le samouraï, sorte de soldat détenteur de privilèges et de terres, était un noble guerrier autorisé à porter l'épée et l'armure sur le champ de bataille et dans la vie civile. Les samouraïs consacraient leur vie au maniement de leur sabre, la *katana*. L'éthique du samouraï exalte le devoir et le sens du sacrifice, qu'elle place même au-dessus de la vie du guerrier lui-même et de l'obéissance qu'il doit à son seigneur féodal et à l'empereur.

De samoerai, een soort soldaat met privileges en land, was een edele krijger met het recht om een zwaard en harnas te dragen op het slagveld en in het dagelijks leven. Samoerai bekwaamden zich hun leven lang in het hanteren van hun katana. De code van de samoerai benadrukte plicht en opoffering, zelfs ten koste van hun leven, en gehoorzaamheid aan de feodale heer en keizer.

Shape_Form_Forme_Vorm

Sketch the internal structure of the figure in a simple pose, with the back axis almost vertical, the shoulders and hips parallel.

Skizziere die innere Struktur der Figur in einfacher Haltung. Die Rückenachse ist nahezu vertikal, Schultern und Hüfte parallel.

Dessinez la structure interne du personnage dans une pose simple, axe du dos pratiquement vertical, et épaules et hanches parallèles.

Schets de inwendige structuur van de figuur in een simpele houding met de as van de rug bijna verticaal en de schouders en heupen evenwijdig.

...eping in mind the ...oulders-and-hip axis, ...d with the feet in ...rspective, overlap the ...apes that are ...eshortened.

Die perspektivisch gezeichneten Körperteile überschneiden einander, vergiss dabei jedoch nicht die Achse zwischen Schulter und Hüfte sowie die Haltung der Füße.

En gardant à l'esprit l'axe des épaules et des hanches, et avec les pieds en perspective, superposez les formes raccourcies.

Laat de verkorte vormen elkaar overlappen, maar let daarbij op de as van schouders en heupen en houd de voeten in perspectief.

Anatomy_Anatomie_Anatomie_Anatomie

Choose a relaxed pose and lower the perspective slightly in order to highlight the character's confident, sideways stance.

Wähle eine entspannte Position und eine etwas niedriger angesetzte Perspektive, um die selbstbewusst wirkende seitliche Haltung der Figur zu betonen.

Choisissez une pose détendue et abaissez légèrement la perspective de manière à mettre en valeur le semi profil plutôt hardi du personnage.

Kies een ontspannen houding en verlaag he perspectief enigszins om de zelfverzekerde zijwaarts gedraaide pose te accentueren.

ake a free-spirited,
venturer Samurai,
ding items such as
e neck scarf and the
bons tied as
istbands to the
nono.

Unterstreiche die
unkonventionelle,
abenteuerliche
Einstellung des Samurai
durch Elemente wie das
Halstuch und die
Armbänder.

Donnez de l'audace et
de l'indépendance
d'esprit à votre
samouraï en ajoutant
des éléments tels que
l'écharpe et les rubans
attachés à la ceinture
du kimono.

Teken de samoerai als
een avonturier met een
vrije geest. Voeg
details, zoals de sjaal
en de als armbanden
omgebonden linten,
aan de kimono toe.

Draw in the outlines of shadows to give the kimono volume, using large, regular patches that fall vertically on the heavy fabric.

Der Kimono erhält Volumen durch die Schatten aus großen, regelmäßigen Elementen, die vertikal an dem schweren Stoff entlang verlaufen.

Dessinez les contours des ombres afin de donner du volume au kimono, en utilisant de larges patches réguliers qui tombent verticalement sur le tissu pesant

Breng de contouren v schaduwen aan om de kimono volume te gevenmet grote, regelmatige vlakken c verticaal op de zware stof vallen.

del the figure with
dows and light
ections and color
kimono in
ditional black, but
ke the scarf a
ant color.

Modelliere die Figur
mithilfe von Schatten
und Licht. Der Kimono
ist traditionell Schwarz,
der Schal jedoch erhält
eine lebhafte Farbe.

Modelez la figure à
l'aide de reflets
d'ombres et de lumière,
coloriez le kimono en
noir classique, mais
donnez à l'écharpe un
coloris très vif.

Geef de figuur vorm
met schaduwen en
lichtreflecties en maak
de kimono traditioneel
zwart, maar geef de
sjaal een felle kleur.

WATER NYMPH

ater nymphs are graceful and kind lake
ries. Larger than their forest cousins and
ore similar to sea animals than insects,
ey are usually seen jumping in the water
id fluttering their wings. Their clothes are
ade of polished shells and very shiny
ements from the ocean floor. Their legs
ways end in a beautifully colored fish tail.

Wassernymphen sind grazile, liebenswürdige
See-Elfen. Ihre Gestalt ist größer als die von
Waldelfen und ähnelt eher Seetieren als
Insekten. Sie bewegen sich schnell und
elegant im Wasser und flattern dabei mit
ihren Flügeln. Ihre Kleidung besteht aus
polierten Muscheln und glitzernden Objekten
vom Meeresboden. Die Beine der
Wassernymphen enden in einem
wunderschönen bunten Fischschwanz.

s naïades sont de gracieuses et gentilles
es des eaux. Plus grandes que leurs
usines des forêts et ressemblant
vantage à des animaux marins qu'à des
ectes, on les voit généralement bondir
ns l'eau et battre des ailes. Leurs
tements se composent de coquillages polis
d'éléments étincelants provenant du fond
l'océan. Leurs jambes se terminent
ijours par une belle queue de poisson
lticolore.

Waternimfen zijn gracieuze, vriendelijke
meerelfen. Ze zijn groter dan hun
soortgenoten in het bos en lijken meer op
zeedieren dan op insecten. Meestal zie je ze
in het water springen en met hun vleugels
fladderen. Hun kleren zijn gemaakt van
gepolijste schelpen en glimmende
voorwerpen van de zeebodem. De benen
eindigen altijd in een prachtig gekleurde
vissenstaart.

Shape_Form_Forme_Vorm

Draw her legs as a base for the tail. Sketch all of the drawing's compositional elements.

Die Beine bilden die Basis für den Fischschwanz. Skizziere alle Elemente der Zeichnung.

Dessinez ses jambes comme une base pour la queue. Esquissez tous les éléments de la composition.

Teken de benen als basis voor de staart. Schets alle compositi elementen van de tekening.

Add volume to her legs in order to draw the tail correctly. We must always respect depth when foreshortening a figure.

Gib den Beinen Volumen, um einen korrekt gezeichneten Schwanz zu erhalten. Beim perspektivischen Zeichnen ist die Tiefe besonders wichtig.

Ajoutez du volume aux jambes de façon à pouvoir dessiner la queue correctement. Vous devez toujours respecter la profondeur en rétrécissant une figure.

Geef de benen meer volume, zodat je de staart goed kunt tekenen. Let altijd op de diepte als je een figuur verkort.

Anatomy_Anatomie_Anatomie_Anatomie

Human legs transform into a fish tail. To make it look right, study the real thing.
Draw her belly button from a three-quarter view.

Die menschlichen Beine gehen in einen Fischschwanz über. Orientiere dich an der Realität, um ein wirklichkeitsgetreues Aussehen zu erhalten. Zeichne den Bauchnabel aus einer Dreiviertel-Ansicht.

Des jambes humaines se transforment en queue de poisson. Pour que ça ait l'air vrai, étudiez la réalité. Dessinez-lui un nombril vu de trois-quarts.

Mensenbenen veranderen in een vissenstaart. Kijk goed hoe echte vissenstaarten eruitzien. Teken de navel in driekwart aanzicht.

r accessories and
thing depict marine
, so draw coral
ulder pads, a snail
her skirt and scale-
vered armor.

Accessoires und
Kleidung stammen aus
der Meereswelt:
Schulterpolster aus
Korallen, ein
Schneckengehäuse als
Rock und eine
schuppenbedeckte
Rüstung.

Ses accessoires et ses
vêtements doivent
évoquer la vie marine ;
vous lui ferez donc des
épaulettes en corail, un
escargot en guise de
jupe et une armure
couverte d'écailles.

De accessoires en
kleding zijn gebaseerd
op het leven in de zee:
koralen
schoudervullingen, een
slak als rok en een
geschubde
wapenrusting.

Lighting_Licht_Éclairage_Licht

Pay attention to the way transparency affects other elements. Delineate the darker areas of the metallic pieces.

Achte vor allem auf die transparenten Bestandteile und ihre Auswirkung auf andere Elemente. Grenze die dunklen Bereiche der Metallteile ab.

Prenez garde à la manière dont la transparence affecte d'autres éléments. Délinéer les zones sombres des pièces métalliques.

Let goed op hoe transparantie andere elementen beïnvloedt Omlijn de donkere gedeelten van de metalen stukken.

contrast the
coldness of the blue
and metallic tones, use
warm color for the
skin so she radiates
tality and happiness.

Um das kühle Blau und
die metallischen
Farbtöne
hervorzuheben, eignen
sich warme Töne für
die Haut. Diese
strahlen Lebendigkeit
und Fröhlichkeit aus.

En opposition à la
froideur du bleu et des
tons métalliques,
utilisez une couleur
chaude pour la peau,
afin que le personnage
irradie de vitalité et de
bonheur.

Geef de huid een
warme kleur die met de
kille blauwe en metallic
tinten contrasteert,
zodat de nimf levens-
lust en blijdschap
uitstraalt.

ADVENTURESS

is highly sensual woman who is equally
arismatic and able, capable of overcoming
dversities and on many occasions with far
ore success than her male counterparts,
s known how to capture the attention of a
oad range of public: from boys who are
xious to see their heroine move her
rves, to girls who view her as an icon they
n identify with.

Diese sinnliche, charismatische und
intelligente Heldin bezwingt zahlreiche Übel,
und dies tut sie häufig mit größerem Erfolg
als ihre männlichen Zeitgenossen. Sie weiß
genau, wie sie die Aufmerksamkeit auf sich
lenkt: Die Jungs lieben die Kurven ihrer
Kämpferin, die Mädchen sehen in ihr ein
Vorbild, dem sie nacheifern können.

femme hyper sensuelle, qui allie charisme
aptitude à surmonter l'adversité, avec
uvent plus de réussite que son homologue
asculin, a su captiver l'attention d'un large
cteur du public : aussi bien garçons
sireux de voir bouger les courbes de leur
roïne, que des filles qui perçoivent en elle
modèle auquel s'identifier.

Deze zeer sensuele vrouw, die even
charismatisch als bekwaam is en vaak met
veel meer succes dan haar mannelijke
tegenhangers tegenslagen kan overwinnen, is
geliefd bij een breed publiek: jongens
bewonderen de welvingen van hun heldin en
meisjes zien haar als hun grote voorbeeld.

Shape_Form_Forme_Vorm

A dynamic pose properly transmits the essence of her adventurous spirit. Here her strength is held in the curve of her back.

Eine dynamische Körperhaltung steht für die Abenteuerlust der Figur. Der gebogene Rücken drückt Kraft und Energie aus.

Une pose dynamique transmet parfaitement l'essence de son esprit aventurier. Ici, la force réside dans la cambrure de son dos.

Een dynamische pose vangt de essentie van de avontuurlijke geest van de vrouw. Haar kracht komt hier tot uitdrukking in de welving van haar rug.

We'll be careful when drawing her breasts, hips and foreshortened arm since these areas give this character her striking appeal.

Achte beim Zeichnen besonders auf die Brüste, Hüften und den vorderen Arm. Diese Körperteile geben der Figur ihre Ausstrahlung.

Soyez minutieux en dessinant sa poitrine, ses hanches et son bras rétréci : ce sont eux qui donnent au personnage son pouvoir de séduction.

Teken vooral de borsten, heupen en verkorte arm met grote zorg, want die delen geven dit personage haar grote aantrekkingskracht.

Anatomy_Anatomie_Anatomie_Anatomie

We'll define her body with clean, dynamic lines that reinforce her movement. Then we'll give her some rudimentary facial features.

Klare, dynamische Linien betonen die Bewegung. Deute nun die Gesichtszüge an.

On définira son corps à l'aide de lignes nettes et dynamiques capables de renforcer le mouvement. Puis on lui donnera des traits rudimentaires.

We zetten het lichaam neer met duidelijke, dynamische lijnen die haar beweging accentueren. Daarna brengen we schetsmatig enkele gelaatstrekken aan.

r clothes depend on
gesture and the
ovement we are
ing to capture. For
s reason, other than
more rigid elements
ch as her boots), the
maining accessories
uld emit strength
d speed.

Die Kleidung der Figur
wird an die Dynamik
von Gestik und
Körperhaltung
angepasst. Daher
sollten auch die übrigen
Accessoires (abgesehen
von unbeweglichen
Elementen wie den
Stiefeln) die kraftvolle,
schnelle Bewegung
aufnehmen.

Ses vêtements
dépendent de la posture
et du mouvement que
l'on tente de reproduire.
Aussi, à part les
éléments rigides
(comme les bottes),
il doit émaner des
accessoires une
sensation de force
et de vitesse.

De kleren volgen de
beweging. Om die
reden moeten de
overige accessoires,
anders dan de meer
starre elementen (zoals
haar laarzen), kracht en
snelheid uitstralen.

Lighting_Licht_Éclairage_Licht

The light focus, located halfway between frontal and zenithal, allows us to focus on details such as her skin and her shadow.

Durch den Lichteinfall von vorne oben können wir Details wie die Haut und den Schattenwurf betonen.

La source de lumière, à mi-chemin entre frontale et zénithale, permet de se concentrer sur des détails tels que la peau du personnage et son ombre.

Dankzij het licht dat van schuin bovenaf komt, komen details als de huid en schaduw goed naar voren.

'll bestow special
sonality by selecting
color of her hair
jacket, which has
ning in common
typical leather.

Individualität erhält die
Figur durch die Farbe
der Haare und der
Jacke, die nicht aus
gewöhnlichem Leder
gefertigt ist.

On lui donnera une
personnalité
particulière en
choisissant la couleur
de ses cheveux et de
sa veste, qui n'a rien de
commun avec du cuir
classique.

We geven de
avonturierster extra
persoonlijkheid met de
kleur van haar haar en
haar jasje, dat niets
gemeen heeft met
normaal leer.

Shading_Schatten_Ombres_Schaduw

Some white areas will accentuate the action so she appears to be sweating, and then we'll add darker shades to the shaded areas.

Füge nun weiße Bereiche hinzu, die den Schweiß auf der Haut unserer Heldin darstellen, und schattiere die dunkleren Stellen.

Un certain nombre de zones blanches accentueront l'action : elle aura ainsi l'air d'être en sueur. Ensuite, on ajoutera des nuances plus sombres aux zones grisées.

Een paar witte vlakke accentueren de actie zodat het lijkt of ze zweet. Daarna voorz we de beschaduwde delen van donkerder tinten.

'll use light colors on
glasses and face in
eral and finish with
shadow on the floor
the light orange
o.

Helle Farben
dominieren das Gesicht
und die Brille; der hell-
orange Umriss und der
Schatten auf dem
Boden runden die
Zeichnung ab.

Utilisez des couleurs
légères pour les
lunettes et le visage en
général, puis finissez
par l'ombre portée sur
le sol et le léger halo
orange.

We geven haar bril en
gezicht lichte kleuren
en eindigen met de
schaduw op de grond
en de lichtoranje
lichtkrans.

KNIGHT

e knight is characterized by great bravery,
 we will show him after having slain a
agon, which he has under his feet.
eanwhile, it looks as if a new threat is
proaching and he's waiting for it. We'll
ow this by using a movement of tension.
e knight must reflect, through his body
d facial expression, the uncertainty and
xiety of the moment.

Der Ritter zeichnet sich vor allem durch Mut
aus; daher steht er auf unserer Zeichnung
auf einem durch ihn getöteten Drachen. Er
scheint auf die nächste Bedrohung zu
warten, der er sich stellen kann. Dies
drücken wir durch die gespannte, in der
Bewegung verharrende Körperhaltung aus. In
der Gestik und Mimik der Figur spiegelt sich
die Gefahr des Moments wider.

chevalier se caractérise par son extrême
avoure ; aussi le montrerons-nous venant
 terrasser le dragon, qui gît sous ses
ds. Mais une nouvelle menace semble
nnoncer et il l'attend de pied ferme. Nous
ntrerons cela à l'aide d'un mouvement de
sion. Le chevalier doit refléter, par son
rps et l'expression de son visage,
certitude et l'angoisse du moment.

De ridder wordt gekenmerkt door grote
dapperheid, dus beelden we hem af met een
draak onder zijn voeten die hij net heeft
gedood. Ondertussen is het alsof hij een
nieuw gevaar voelt aankomen. Dat tonen we
door een spanning in het lichaam. Uit het
lichaam en de gezichtsuitdrukking van de
ridder moeten de onzekerheid en spanning
van het moment spreken.

Shape_Form_Forme_Vorm

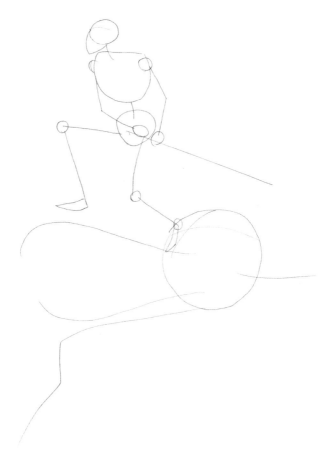

Sketch, with few lines, the dragon's head.

Skizziere mit wenigen Linien den Drachenkopf.

Esquissez à grands traits la tête du dragon.

Schets met een paar lijnen de kop van de draak.

e feet rest on the
agon's head. The
dy is half-turned and
e arms are clutching
e sword, about to
sheathe it.

Die Füße stehen auf
dem Kopf des Drachen.
Der Körper befindet
sich in einer halben
Drehung und die Hände
umklammern das
Schwert, jederzeit
bereit, es zu ziehen.

Les pieds reposent sur
la tête du dragon. Le
corps est tourné à demi
et les bras empoignent
l'épée, prêts à la tirer
de son fourreau.

De voeten rusten op de
drakenkop. Het lichaam
is halfgedraaid en de
armen staan op het
punt het zwaard te
trekken.

Anatomy_Anatomie_Anatomie_Anatomie

At a slight dip, the collarbone accentuates the U-shape. We'll depict an expression of rage and defiance.

Das U-förmige Schlüsselbein spiegelt in seiner Biegung die Körperhaltung wider. Wut und Kampfeslust dominieren die gesamte Zeichnung.

Légèrement infléchie, la clavicule accentue la forme en U. On donnera au personnage une expression de farouche défi.

De sleutelbeenderen buigen iets door, wat de U-vorm versterkt. We geven de ridder ee woedende, tartende uitdrukking.

...e tails and cloak
...llow the wind. Apply
...e clothes layer upon
...yer, with creases in
...e direction of the
...int of tension.

Die Bänder und der
Umhang flattern im
Wind. Zeichne die
Kleidung Schicht für
Schicht und deute
Falten in der
Verlaufsrichtung an.

Les pans de la cape
flottent au vent.
Appliquez les
vêtements couche à
couche, avec des plis
en direction du point
de tension.

De slippen en mantel
volgen de wind. Breng
de kleren laag voor
laag aan, met vouwen
in de richting van
het spannings-punt.

Lighting_Licht_Éclairage_Licht

We will draw the folds of the clothes and their shadows. Also, consider lighting with two different light sources at the same time.

Nun füge weitere Falten und Schatten an den richtigen Stellen hinzu, der Lichteinfall erfolgt aus zwei unterschiedlichen Quellen.

On dessinera les replis des vêtements et leurs ombres. Et on envisagera l'illumination avec deux différentes sources de lumière à la fois.

Nu tekenen we de plooien van de kleren en de schaduwen en gebruiken we twee verschillende lichtbronnen tegelijk.

e'll give him a
ntastical hair color,
en finish the trousers
:h some spots and
ripes and draw the
:ales directly with
lor.

Verleihe dem Haar eine
Fantasiefarbe. Füge
dem Stoff der Hose
einige Punkte und
Streifen hinzu und male
die Drachenschuppen
direkt mit Farbe.

On lui donnera une
teinte de cheveux
fantastique, puis on
finira les pantalons en
ajoutant des tâches et
des bandes, après quoi
on dessinera les
écailles directement à
la couleur.

We geven de ridder een
bijzondere kleur haar
en werken dan de
broek af met wat
stippen en strepen en
tekenen de schubben
van de draak meteen in
kleur.

VALKYRIA

e perfect combination of almost divine
auty and strength make the Valkyria an
sily recognizable character within the
tensive gallery of heroines inhabiting the
rld of *manga*. With long platinum blonde
ir that is as shiny as their shining armor,
ey are among the most epic and romantic
roines around. She is a true symbiosis of
licacy and heroism.

Die perfekte Kombination aus einer fast
göttlichen Schönheit und Strenge machen
die „Valkyria" zu einem leicht
identifizierbaren Charakter in der Galerie der
Manga-Heldinnen. Mit ihrem langen
platinblonden Haar, das ebenso glänzt wie
ihre Rüstung, ist sie eine der mutigsten und
romantischsten Heldinnen – die perfekte
Symbiose aus delikater Schönheit und
Heldentum.

lliance parfaite de la beauté quasiment
ine et de la force fait de la Walkyrie un
rsonnage aisément reconnaissable dans la
erie fort étendue des héroïnes de l'univers
manga. Avec sa longue chevelure blond
tine, aussi brillante que son armure
ntillante, c'est l'une des héroïnes épiques
romantiques par excellence : un véritable
ncrétisme de délicatesse et d'héroïsme.

Door de perfecte combinatie van bijna
goddelijke schoonheid en kracht is de
Walkure een heel herkenbaar personage in
de uitgebreide galerij van heldinnen die de
wereld van manga bevolken. Met hun lange
platinablonde haar, dat even stralend glanst
als hun wapenrusting, behoren ze tot de
meest heroïsche en romantische heldinnen
die er zijn. De Walkure is een volmaakte
samensmelting van gratie en heldendom.

Shape_Form_Forme_Vorm

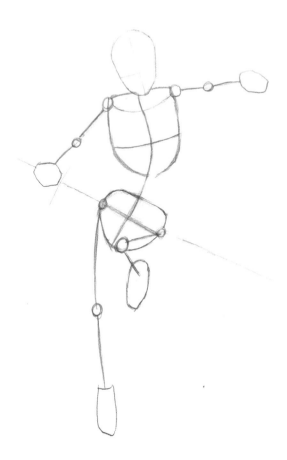

We must foreshorten her arms and legs, and adjust the position of her waist, which is conditioned by the line of her spinal column.

Arme und Beine werden perspektivisch gezeichnet, darauf abgestimmt ist die Hüfte, deren Haltung von der Rückenposition abhängt.

Il vous faut rétrécir ses bras et ses jambes, et ajuster la position de sa ceinture, qui dépend de la ligne de sa colonne vertébrale.

We moeten de armen en benen verkorten e middel aanpassen, di bepaald wordt door d lijn van de wervelkolo

e Valkyria must have athletic build that is elte at the same e; we're not aiming a woman with a uptuous body.

Der Körperbau der Valkyria ist athletisch und gleichzeitig anmutig – üppige Kurven sind hier nicht die Hauptsache.

La Walkyrie doit avoir un corps athlétique et svelte à la fois ; on ne cherche pas ici à dessiner une femme aux courbes voluptueuses.

De bouw van de Walkure moet atletisch en slank tegelijk zijn; we streven hier niet naar een vrouw met een voluptueus lichaam.

Anatomy_Anatomie_Anatomie_Anatomie

We'll give her large eyes, with hair flying according to her movement, and then define her anatomy without making her too muscular.

Gib unserer Heldin große Augen und in der Bewegung flatterndes Haar; definiere anschließend den Körper, ohne ihn zu muskulös erscheinen zu lassen.

Nous lui donnerons de grands yeux, des cheveux qui virevoltent au gré de ses mouvements, puis nous définirons son anatomie sans trop la muscler.

We geven haar grote ogen, met wapperend haar dat haar bewegi volgt, en tekenen dan haar anatomie zonder haar te gespierd te maken.

think about how her
cape hangs and how it
ties in to the heroine's
movements, while
looking for motifs that
allude to mythology.

Achte darauf, wie ihr
Umhang herabhängt
und der Bewegung folgt
und überlege dir
Motive, die auf die
Mythologie anspielen.

Pensez à la manière
dont la cape tombe et
épouse les
mouvements de
l'héroïne, et recherchez
des motifs évocateurs
de la mythologie.

Bedenk hoe haar cape
hangt en hoe deze
meegeeft met de
bewegingen van de
heldin. Probeer
mythologisch getinte
motieven te vinden.

Lighting_Licht_Éclairage_Licht

Here we have natural lighting where the shadows are projected on the lower areas of objects. We should focus on her chrome armor.

Die natürliche Beleuchtung sorgt dafür, dass sich der Schatten an der Unterseite der Objekte befindet. Schenke der metallisch schimmernden Rüstung besondere Aufmerksamkeit.

Nous avons ici un éclairage naturel où les ombres sont projetées au bas des objets. Il faut se concentrer sur l'armure chromée.

We hebben hier natuurlijk licht, waarbij de schaduwen op de onderkant van de voorwerpen worden geworpen. We concentreren ons vooral op de chrome wapenrusting.

e'll use not very
turated pastels,
cept for the cape
ich will be left in the
ckground without
ing any of its impact.

Verwende ungesättigte
Pastelltöne, außer für
den Umhang, der im
Hintergrund
eindrucksvoll flattert.

On utilisera des pastels
peu saturés, sauf pour
la cape qui sera laissée
au second plan, sans
pour autant perdre de
sa vigueur.

We gebruiken niet erg
verzadigde pasteltinten,
behalve voor de cape,
die op de achtergrond
blijft zonder ook maar
enigszins aan impact in
te boeten.

Shading_Schatten_Ombres_Schaduw

Observe how the armor reflects on her skin, hair and outfit. Keep the cape in the background by limiting its reflections.

Die Rüstung spiegelt sich auf der Haut unserer Heldin, während der Umhang im Hintergrund weniger Reflexe erhält.

Observez le miroitement de l'armure sur la peau, les cheveux et les vêtements du personnage. Laissez la cape à l'arrière-plan en en limitant les reflets.

Let op hoe de wapen rusting reflecteert op de huid, het haar en kleding. Houd de cap op de achtergrond do zijn reflecties beperk te houden.

inting a red border
th a dappling effect
ound the Valkyria
ves her movement.
stly, we'll contour her
m and sword.

Ein roter, gesprenkelter
Umriss unterstreicht
die Bewegung der
Valkyria. Schließlich
erhalten Arm und
Schwert Konturen.

Peindre une bordure
rouge avec un effet
moutonné autour de la
Walkyrie lui donnera du
mouvement. Pour finir,
soulignez le contour de
son bras et de l'épée.

Een wazige rode rand
om de Walkure heen
suggereert beweging.
Ten slotte geven we
haar arm en zwaard
een contour.

he Baddies
Die Bösen
Les Méchants
e slechteriken

DEVIL

evils are gigantic and horrible, with fangs
nd horns that come out of their body and
erve as lethal weapons. His face must
xpress the very personification of evil with a
rcastic, wicked laugh. Our character is
tting down, practically sideways in an S-
naped vertical composition. This is a good
pportunity to practice a half-human, half-
upernatural anatomy.

Teufel sind riesig und Furcht einflößend,
Reißzähne, Krallen und Hörner dienen ihnen
als Waffe. Im Gesicht des sarkastisch und
bösartig lachenden Teufels spiegelt sich das
Böse wider. Er sitzt in der Hocke, in einer
seitlichen, S-förmigen Körperhaltung. Hier
kannst du das Zeichnen einer halb
menschlichen, halb übernatürlichen
Anatomie üben.

es démons, gigantesques et horribles, ont le
rps hérissé de crocs et de cornes ; ils font
fice d'armes létales. Leur face doit être
ncarnation même du mal, avec un rictus
rdonique et abject. Notre personnage est
sis, pratiquement de côté, dans une
mposition verticale en forme de S. C'est
e bonne occasion de s'entraîner à dessiner
e anatomie mi-humaine, mi-surnaturelle.

Duivels zijn reusachtig en huiveringwekkend
en hebben grote tanden en hoorns uit hun
lichaam groeien die als dodelijke wapens
dienen. Het gezicht moet pure kwaadaardig-
heid uitstralen met een spottende,
boosaardige lach. Ons personage zit bijna
helemaal zijwaarts in een verticale, S-
vormige compositie. Dit is een goede kans
om te oefenen op een half menselijke, half
bovennatuurlijke anatomie.

Shape_Form_Forme_Vorm

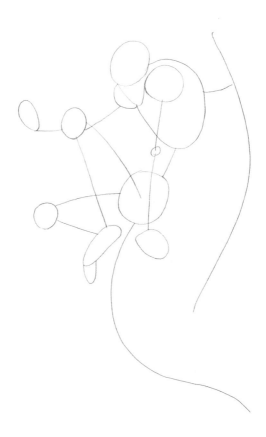

We'll mark a very curved spine, almost in a fetal position with an S-shaped composition.

Deute das gebogene Rückgrat und die kauernde Körperhaltung durch die S-förmige Komposition an.

On ébauchera une colonne vertébrale très courbée, presque en position fœtale, avec une composition en forme de S.

We geven de duivel een heel kromme ruggengraat – haast een foetushouding met een S-vormige lijn.

wings protrude
n both sides of the
k. The figure is
ing on skulls, which
will initially draw
ng spheres.

Die Flügel befinden sich
am seitlichen Rücken.
Die Figur sitzt auf
Totenköpfen, die wir zu
Beginn durch Kreise
andeuten.

Les ailes font saillie de
chaque côté du dos. La
figure est assise sur
des crânes, que l'on
dessinera à partir de
sphères.

De vleugels steken uit
aan weerszijden van de
rug. De figuur zit op
schedels, die we in
eerste instantie met
cirkels weergeven.

Anatomy_Anatomie_Anatomie_Anatomie

His muscles are similar to humans' but with bony horns and a cartilage crest. Sharp teeth and wide eyes mark his evil expression.

Die Muskeln dieses Teufels ähneln denen von Menschen. Knochige Hörner, ein knorpeliger Kamm, scharfe Zähne und ein stechender Blick sorgen für das teuflische Aussehen.

Ses muscles sont analogues à ceux des humains, mais pourvus de cornes osseuses et d'une crête cartilagineuse. Des dents acérées et de gros yeux caractérisent son expression démoniaque.

De spieren zijn als di van mensen, maar da met hoorns en een kraakbenen kam. Scherpe tanden en grote ogen geven de duivel een boosaardi uitdrukking.

s clothes fit tight ound his body and his cessoires are based thorns and horns.

Die Kleidung sitzt eng am Körper und ist mit Stacheln und Hörnern versehen.

Les vêtements épousent le corps et les accessoires s'inspirent de cornes et d'aiguillons.

De kleren sluiten nauw om het lichaam en de accessoires zijn gebaseerd op doorns en hoorns.

Lighting_Licht_Éclairage_Licht

The shadows fall on the upper part of the figures, as the light comes from below. Notice the rough texture of the horns.

Das von unten kommende Licht wirft Schatten auf die Oberseite des Körpers. Achte dabei auf die raue Oberfläche der Hörner.

Les ombres tombent sur la partie supérieure des figures, tandis que la lumière vient d'en dessous. Remarquez la texture rugueuse des cornes.

Doordat het licht van onderaf komt, vallen schaduwen op het bovenste gedeelte va de figuren. Let op he ruwe oppervlak van c hoorns.

d tones predominate they create an ernal atmosphere. e skin's texture ould convey a nsation of hardness.

Rote Farbtöne dominieren die Szene und schaffen eine diabolische Atmosphäre. Die Haut wirkt hart und spröde.

Les tons rouges prédominent et créent une atmosphère infernale. La texture de la peau doit transmettre une sensation de dureté.

Rode tinten overheersen, omdat die een helse sfeer creëren. Het huidoppervlak moet hardheid suggereren.

ROMANTIC GOTHIC

Whether it's because of Victorian poetry and horror stories, or because of the mixture of fatal attraction and melancholy that characterize tales where humans fall in love with monsters, ghosts or other similar creatures, these stories are dark, intense and passionate. The monster tends to appear to us as just another victim of love, unable to escape his destiny.

Inspiriert durch Gedichte und Horrorgeschichten aus der Romantik, eine Komposition aus verhängnisvoller Begierde und Melancholie sowie Menschen, die sich in Monster, Geister oder andere Kreaturen verlieben, sind Kennzeichen dieser dunklen, leidenschaftlichen Geschichten. Das Monster ist häufig ebenfalls ein Opfer der Liebe, das seinem Schicksal nicht entfliehen kann.

Soit à cause de la poésie victorienne et des histoires d'horreur, soit du mélange d'attraction fatale et de mélancolie qui caractérise les récits où des hommes s'éprennent de monstres, de fantômes ou de créatures similaires, ces histoires sont toujours sombres, intenses et passionnées. Le monstre y apparaît souvent, lui aussi, comme une victime de l'amour, incapable d'échapper à son destin.

Of het nu vanwege de victoriaanse poëzie en griezelverhalen is, of vanwege de combinatie van noodlottige aantrekkingskracht en melancholie die verhalen kenmerken waarin mensen verliefd worden op monsters, geesten en dergelijke wezens, deze verhalen zijn duister, intens en hartstochtelijk. Het monster komt ons voor als het zoveelste slachtoffer van de liefde dat niet kan ontkomen aan zijn lot.

Shape_Form_Forme_Vorm

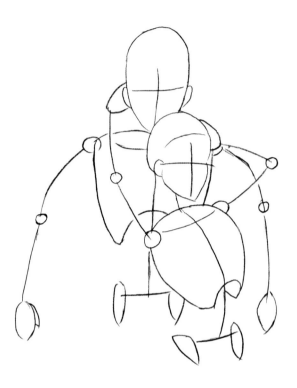

Draw the characters in their theatrical poses, as if frozen in a time and context full of intensity.

Die Figuren befinden sich in einer theatralischen Haltung, wie erstarrt in einer leidenschaftlichen Szene.

Dessinez les personnages dans leurs poses théâtrales, comme s'ils étaient figés dans une époque et un contexte lourds d'intensité.

Teken de personages theatrale poses, vol intensiteit en alsof de tijd is stilgezet.

low the atmosphere
the setting and draw
n and elegant
ures.

Zeichne schlanke,
elegante Charaktere,
passend zur
Atmosphäre.

Respectez l'atmosphère
de la scène et dessinez
des silhouettes sveltes
et élégantes.

Sluit aan bij de sfeer
van de setting en teken
slanke, elegante
figuren.

Anatomy_Anatomie_Anatomie_Anatomie

Characters from this period appear listless, with delicate features, such as elaborate eyes that mirror the character's emotions.

Aus dieser Zeit stammende Figuren erscheinen fragil und empfindsam, so spiegeln sich in ihren Augen häufig ihre Gefühle wider.

Indolents en apparence, les personnages de cette période ont des traits délicats, et notamment des yeux subtilement dessinés qui reflètent leurs émotions.

Personages uit deze periode komen lusteloos over en hebben fijne trekken, zoals complexe ogen die de emoties van h personage weerspiegelen.

ng suits and dresses,
ls and other
rments with lots of
eats and folds are
mmon in romantic-
thic stories.

Flatternde, mit
Rüschen, Plissee und
Falten ausgestattete
Anzüge und Kleider
sind in romantischen
Gothic-Storys weit
verbreitet.

Longs habits, grandes
robes, jabots et autres
vêtements agrémentés
de volants et de plis,
sont des parures
courantes du roman
gothique.

Lange gewaden en
jurken, franje en andere
kledingstukken met tal
van vouwen en plooien
komen veel voor in
romantisch-gotische
verhalen.

Lighting_Licht_Éclairage_Licht

Gloomy lighting without strong contrast is best for this scene. Light and shadow are distinguishable in an expressionist way.

Diese Szene sollte in dämmriges Licht ohne starke Kontraste getaucht sein. Licht und Schatten wirken fast expressionistisch.

Une illumination ténébreuse, sans contraste fort, convient mieux à cette scène. La lumière et l'ombre se différencient de manière expressionniste.

Schemerlicht zonder sterk contrast is het beste voor dit tafereel Licht en schaduw late zich op een expressio nistische manier onderscheiden.

e woman's dress has
rish colors and many
etails, while the man's
oak is in sedate
olors and rich-looking
oric.

Grelle Farben und
zahlreiche Details
zeichnen das Kleid der
Frau aus, während der
aus edlem Stoff
gefertigte Mantel des
Mannes in gedeckten
Farben gehalten ist.

La robe de la femme se
caractérise par des
couleurs voyantes et
une foule de détails,
tandis que l'étoffe
somptueuse de la cape
de l'homme affiche des
couleurs soyeuses.

De jurk van de vrouw
heeft felle kleuren en
veel details, terwijl de
mantel van de man
stemmig gekleurd is en
gemaakt van prachtige
stof.

TROLL

Trolls are an anthropomorphic race. Sometimes they are diabolical giants who look like ogres; other times they are tamed savages who look more like men. They live in low hills or mounds and have a tendency to kidnap humans. Often they look aboriginal with enormous ears and noses, and are ugly and foul-smelling. They personify the dangers of the forest.

Trolle sind anthropomorphe Gestalten, die manchmal als teuflische Ungeheuer, manchmal als eher zahme, menschenähnliche Wilde auftreten. Sie leben in Bergen oder Hügeln und rauben gerne Menschen. Ihr urtümliches Aussehen wird häufig von riesigen Ohren und Nasen, Hässlichkeit und Gestank begleitet. Sie verkörpern die Gefahren des Waldes.

Les trolls sont une race d'humanoïdes. Parfois, ils adoptent l'apparence de géants diaboliques comparables à des ogres, d'autres fois de sauvages apprivoisés ressemblant davantage à des hommes. Ils vivent sous des terres ou des collines, et ils ont tendance à ravir les humains. D'apparence souvent primitive, affligés de nez et d'oreilles démesurés, ils sont laids et malodorants. Ils incarnent les dangers de la forêt.

Trollen zijn een antropomorf ras. Soms zijn het duivelse reuzen, soms getemde wilden die meer op mensen lijken. Ze leven onder heuvels en ontvoeren vaak mensen. Vaak zien ze eruit als ogers met enorme oren en neuzen, zijn ze lelijk en stinken ze. Ze belichamen de gevaren van het bos.

Shape_Form_Forme_Vorm

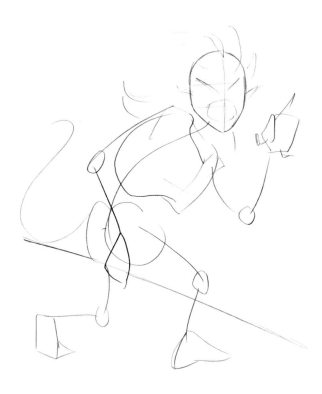

His raised hand holds his prisoner. Break his stride by twisting his upper body as he returns to his chamber.

In der erhobenen Hand des Trolls ist der Gefangene zu erkennen. Sein Schritt wird durch die Drehung des Oberkörpers durchbrochen.

La main levée renferme un prisonnier. Interrompez son enjambée en tordant la partie supérieure de son corps comme s'il rentrait dans sa tanière.

De opgeheven hand houdt de gevangene vast. Onderbreek de gang van de trol door zijn bovenlichaam te draaien terwijl hij teruggaat naar zijn kamer.

s arms are much
ger than normal and
e legs are short and
ong. He is a glutton,
give him a round
ly.

Die Arme sind
überproportional und
die Beine kurz und
kräftig, seiner
Gefräßigkeit verdankt er
einen Kugelbauch.

Ses bras sont plus forts
que la normale ; ses
jambes sont courtes et
trapues. C'est un
glouton, alors faites-lui
un ventre rond.

De armen zijn veel
groter dan normaal en
de benen zijn kort en
sterk. Het is een
veelvraat, dus geef hem
een dikke buik.

Anatomy_Anatomie_Anatomie_Anatomie

He has terribly ugly features with lots of hair on his skin and at the end of his tail and gigantic arms with powerful muscles.

Die Hässlichkeit der Gestalt wird durch borstige Haare auf der Haut und am Schwanz sowie riesige, muskulöse Arme unterstrichen.

Son visage est terriblement laid, avec des poils partout, sur la peau et au bout de la queue ; il a des bras gigantesques aux muscles puissants.

Hij is oerlelijk, heeft heel veel haar op zijn huid en aan zijn staar en hij heeft kolossale armen met krachtige spieren.

e troll wears tribal ornments made of bones and skulls of asts. The frayed rope ggests a prisoner s once tied there.

Der Troll trägt primitiven Schmuck aus Tierknochen und -schädeln. Der abgerissene Strick deutet an, dass daran ein Gefangener befestigt war.

Le troll porte des ornements tribaux faits d'ossements et de crânes d'animaux. La corde effrangée suggère qu'un prisonnier a été ligoté avec.

De trol draagt stamdecoraties van beenderen en dierenschedels. Het gerafelde touw doet vermoeden dat hieraan een gevangene vastgebonden heeft gezeten.

Lighting_Licht_Éclairage_Licht

Place the light so that it completely illuminates his face and exaggerates his expression. This way he'll become truly terrifying.

Platziere das Licht so, dass es das Gesicht komplett beleuchtet und somit die Mimik übertrieben wirken lässt – dadurch wirkt dieses Wesen noch fürchterlicher.

Placez la lumière de façon à ce qu'elle illumine entièrement le visage du troll et en exagère l'expression. Ainsi, il sera vraiment terrifiant.

Plaats het licht zo da het zijn gezicht volled verlicht. Daardoor kri de gelaatsuitdrukking een grotesk karakter wordt hij pas echt angstaanjagend.

strident color of troll's hair makes look even stranger, e his red hat serves a secondary source ttention.

Die grelle Haarfarbe lässt den Troll noch absonderlicher aussehen, während der rote Hut eine zweite Aufmerksamkeitsquelle darstellt.

La couleur criarde de la chevelure du troll lui donne un air encore plus bizarre, tandis que le chapeau rouge tient lieu de point d'attraction subsidiaire.

Door de schreeuwende kleur van zijn haar ziet de trol er nog vreemder uit. Daarnaast trekt ook zijn rode hoed de aandacht.

KELETON

riors who once died on the battlefield till
ar some of their armor or carry their
apons, only now they serve as slaves to
ck magic. It doesn't matter how many
es they fall or are hit, they always get up
go after their enemy. Luckily they can't go
ond these lands since the magic of the
ds of the underworld still isn't strong
ough.

Auf dem Schlachtfeld gefallene Krieger
tragen immer noch Teile ihrer Rüstung oder
Waffen – allerdings sind sie mittlerweile zu
Sklaven der schwarzen Magie geworden. Es
spielt keine Rolle, wie oft sie getötet oder
verletzt werden: Sie stehen immer wieder
auf, um ihren Feind zu verfolgen.
Glücklicherweise sind sie nicht fähig, die
Landesgrenzen zu überschreiten, da die
Herren der Unterwelt noch über zu wenig
Macht verfügen.

tains guerriers morts au champ de
aille portent toujours leur armure ou leurs
es..., l'ennui, c'est qu'ils servent
ormais d'esclaves de magie noire. Ils
vent tomber, se blesser un nombre de
incalculable, peu importe, ils se relèvent
ours pour se lancer à la poursuite de
s ennemis. Heureusement, ils ne peuvent
chir la limite de ces terres : la magie des
tres des enfers n'est pas assez puissante.

Krijgers die ooit op het slagveld gesneuveld
zijn, dragen nog steeds een deel van hun
harnas of hun wapens; alleen dienen ze nu
als slaven van zwarte magie. Hoe vaak ze
ook vallen of getroffen worden, ze staan
altijd weer op om achter hun vijand aan te
gaan. Doordat de magie van de heersers van
de onderwereld nog niet sterk genoeg is,
kunnen ze gelukkig niet voorbij de grenzen
van dit rijk.

Shape_Form_Forme_Vorm

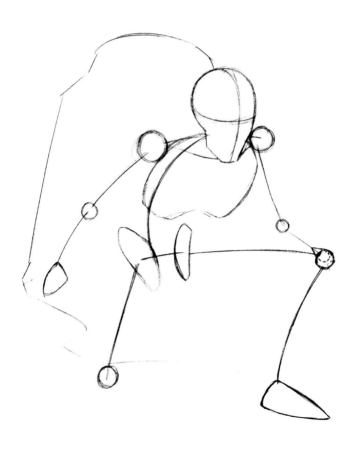

Draw an arched spinal column. Sketch the rest of the pose while considering the resting point.

Zeichne zunächst das gebogene Rückgrat. Skizziere dann den Rest des Körpers und berücksichtige dabei den Ruhepunkt.

Dessinez une colonne vertébrale courbée. Esquissez le reste de la posture tout en considérant le point de repos.

Teken een gebogen wervelkolom. Schets rest van de houding let daarbij op het rustpunt.

etch the volume of
 sword and armor.

Deute die Umrisse von
Schwert und Rüstung
an.

Ébauchez le volume de
l'épée et de l'armure.

Schets het volume van
het zwaard en harnas.

Anatomy_Anatomie_Anatomie_Anatomie

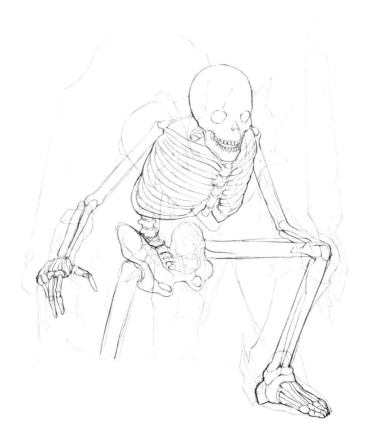

Define the skeleton's skull, hand and foot.

Definiere anschließend Schädel, Hand und Fuß des Skeletts.

Définissez le crâne, la main et le pied du squelette.

Teken de schedel, handen en voet van h geraamte.

ake the armor, sword
d skeleton look worn.
e coat of mail helps
d weight and
ovement. Finish with
tombstone and grave.

Achte darauf, dass
Rüstung, Schwert und
das Skelett selbst
schäbig wirken. Das
Panzerhemd gibt der
Gestalt Gewicht. Füge
einen Grabstein und
das Grab hinzu.

Donnez un aspect usé
à l'armure, à l'épée et
au squelette lui-même.
La cotte de mailles
contribue à accentuer
le poids et le
mouvement. Pour finir,
ajoutez une stèle et
une tombe.

Geef het harnas,
zwaard en geraamte
een versleten uiterlijk.
De maliënkolder voegt
gewicht en beweging
toe. Teken ten slotte
een grafsteen en een
graf.

Lighting_Licht_Éclairage_Licht

The light comes from the front and projects the skeleton's shadow over the tombstone.

Durch das von vorne einfallende Licht fällt der Schatten des Skeletts auf den Grabstein.

La lumière vient de devant et projette l'ombre du squelette sur la pierre tombale.

Het licht komt van voren, waardoor het geraamte een schaduw op de grafsteen werpt

se a variety of tones
n the worn and rusty
etal, with lighter
nes for the darker
eas like the grave and
ner armor.

Verwende verschiedene
Farbtöne für das
abgetragene, rostige
Metall und betone
dunkle Bereiche wie
das Grab und die
Innenseite der Rüstung.

Utilisez une variété de
tons sur le métal usé et
rouillé, avec des
couleurs plus légères
pour les zones plus
sombres comme la
tombe et l'intérieur de
l'armure.

Gebruik diverse tinten
voor het versleten en
roestige metaal en
lichtere tinten voor de
donkere gedeelten,
zoals het graf en de
binnenkant van het
harnas.

PIXIE

xies are a curious race of small, naughty
eings similar to fairies but known to have
oor taste when joking around. They are
mall, with pointy ears and almond-shaped
es, but without wings. They usually dress
 worn-out green clothes. Our pixie will also
e a bit mischievous; surely she's caused
ore than one human to get lost in the
agical garden.

Eine „Pixie" ist ein seltsames, kleines, listiges
Wesen, das Ähnlichkeit mit Elfen hat, aber im
Gegensatz zu diesen dreiste Scherze treibt.
Diese kleinen Gestalten haben spitze Ohren
und mandelförmige Augen, tragen aber keine
Flügel. Gewöhnlich sieht man sie in
abgetragenen grünen Kleidern. Unsere Pixie
wirkt etwas heimtückisch – sicherlich hat sie
dafür gesorgt, dass sich mehr als nur ein
Mensch im magischen Garten verirrt hat.

s *pixies* sont d'étranges petits êtres
alveillants qui ressemblent aux fées mais
nt réputés pour leurs blagues de mauvais
ût. De petite taille, ils ont des oreilles
intues et des yeux en amandes, mais pas
iles. Ils portent généralement des habits
 lambeaux, de couleur verte. Notre *pixie*
ra également un peu malicieuse ; parions
'elle a dû égarer plus d'un homme dans le
din magique.

Elfjes zijn een nieuwsgierig ras van kleine
schavuiten die in tegenstelling tot grotere
elfen weinig smaak aan de dag leggen in hun
grappen. Ze zijn klein en hebben spitse oren
en amandelvormige ogen, maar geen
vleugels. Meestal dragen ze versleten groene
kleren. Ons elfje is ook een beetje
ondeugend: door haar zijn vast en zeker al
verschillende mensen verdwaald in de
magische tuin.

Shape_Form_Forme_Vorm

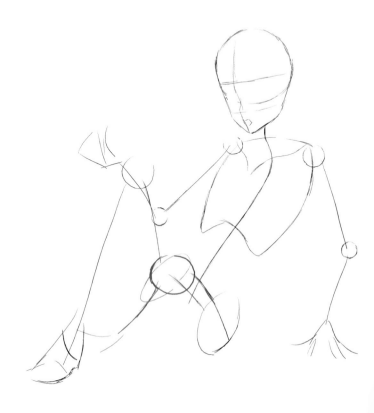

When drawing a character sitting or lying down, mark the resting points for the pose: the buttocks, hand and feet.

Achte beim Zeichnen von sitzenden oder liegenden Charakteren auf die Ruhepunkte: Gesäß, Hand und Füße.

Lorsque vous dessinez un personnage assis ou allongé, marquez les points de repos pour cette posture : les fesses, la main et les pieds.

Als je een zittende of liggende figuur tekent plaats dan het rustpu van de houding bij de billen, hand en voeter

In order to place the character correctly, draw the knee so it's in front of the thighs, with the thighs in front of the hips.

Um die Figur richtig zu positionieren, sollte das Knie vor den Oberschenkeln platziert werden, die Oberschenkel wiederum befinden sich vor der Hüfte.

Afin de placer correctement le personnage, dessinez le genou devant les cuisses, et les cuisses devant les hanches.

Teken, om het personage correct te plaatsen, de knie voor de dijen en de dijen voor de heupen.

Anatomy_Anatomie_Anatomie_Anatomie

Curvaceous lines make her more attractive. Work her fairy facial features and pay attention to her fingers, toes and left leg.

Durch kurvige Linien erhält die Figur mehr Attraktivität. Arbeite ihre elfenhaften Merkmale heraus und achte dabei auf Finger, Zehen und das linke Bein.

Des lignes courbes la rendront plus séduisante. Travaillez les traits de son visage de fée et faites attention à ses doigts de main et de pied, ainsi qu'à sa jambe gauche.

Welvende lijnen make het elfje aantrekkelijk Teken haar elfachtige gelaatstrekken en let goed op haar vingers tenen en linkerbeen.

e pixie uses plants
clothing, so her
tfit is crude, wild and
ring. Find models to
aw the strawberries
alistically.

Die Pixie verarbeitet
Pflanzen zu Kleidung,
daher wirkt ihr Outfit
urtümlich, wild und
gewagt. Verwende
echte Erdbeeren als
Modelle, um die
Früchte realistisch
wirken zu lassen.

La *pixie* utilise des
plantes pour se vêtir ;
ses habits sont donc
grossiers, rustiques et
osés. Trouvez des
modèles pour
représenter les fraises
avec réalisme.

Het elfje kleedt zich
met planten. Haar
kleding is dus grof, wild
en gewaagd. Zoek
voorbeelden om de
aardbeien realistisch
weer te geven.

Lighting_Licht_Éclairage_Licht

Lighting gives the character volume and the background structure, while the shadows from the pixie's hair hide her naughty look.

Die Beleuchtung verleiht der Figur Volumen und gibt dem Hintergrund Struktur, während der Schatten der Haare den listigen Blick verbirgt.

La lumière donne du volume au personnage et à la structure de l'arrière-plan, tandis que les ombres de la chevelure dissimulent le regard malveillant de la *pixie*.

Licht geeft het personage volume en de achtergrond structuur, terwijl de schaduwen van het haar de ondeugende blik van het elfje verbergen.

arm colors make the xie look more tractive and open. se soft colors for the ackground and darker hes for the reground.	Warme Farbtöne lassen das Wesen attraktiv und offen erscheinen. Verwende zurückhaltende Farbtöne für den Hintergrund und dunkle Farben für den Vordergrund.	Des couleurs chaudes rendront la *pixie* plus attirante et aimable. Utilisez des couleurs douces pour l'arrière-plan, et des teintes plus sombres au premier plan.	Met warme kleuren lijkt het elfje aantrekkelijker en opener. Gebruik zachte kleuren voor de achtergrond en donker-der kleuren voor de voor-grond.

MASKED RIDER

e masked rider is generally presented as a
iturn, lonely hero, doomed to roam the
✓ streets on a ghostly bike. His special
form and mask are essential features that
ke him look diabolical and highlight his
k of humanity. The origin of the masked
er is usually related to supernatural events
o the resurrection of a person in search
vengeance.

Der „Masked Rider" (maskierter Fahrer) ist
als schweigsamer, einsamer Held dazu
verdammt, mit seinem geisterhaften
Motorrad die Straßen der Stadt zu
durchstreifen. Seine besondere Uniform und
die Maske sind wichtige Kennzeichen, die
den Fahrer diabolisch erscheinen lassen und
seine Unmenschlichkeit unterstreichen. Das
Auftauchen des Masked Rider steht
normalerweise mit übernatürlichen
Ereignissen oder der Rettung einer Person in
Verbindung. Er ist stets auf der Suche nach
Rache.

motard masqué est généralement
résenté comme un héros taciturne et
taire, condamné à hanter les rues des
es sur une moto fantôme. Son curieux
outrement et son masque font partie
grante de son allure diabolique,
lignant son absence d'humanité. L'origine
motard masqué est d'ordinaire associée à
événements surnaturels, ou à la
urrection d'un être en quête de
geance.

De gemaskerde motorrijder is meestal een
zwijgzame, eenzame held die gedoemd is op
een spookmotor door de straten van de stad
te dolen. Zijn speciale uniform en masker zijn
essentiële elementen die hem een duivels,
niet-menselijk voorkomen geven. De
oorsprong van de gemaskerde motorrijder
hangt meestal samen met bovennatuurlijke
gebeurtenissen of de opwekking van iemand
die uit is op wraak.

Shape_Form_Forme_Vorm

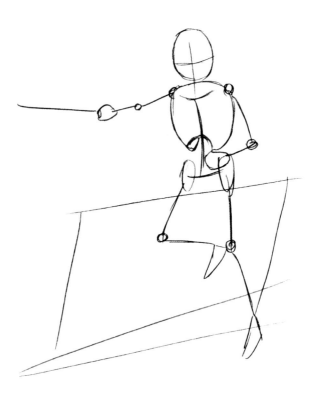

Begin by sketching the ground and bike with a couple of lines to mark the two elements as well as the background perspective.

Skizziere zunächst den Boden und das Motorrad mit wenigen Linien, um sowohl die Position der zwei Elemente als auch die Hintergrundperspektive festzulegen.

Commencez par dessiner le sol et la moto à grands traits pour marquer l'emplacement de ces deux éléments, ainsi que la perspective à l'arrière-plan.

Schets eerst de gro▮ en de motor met ee▮ paar lijnen om de tw▮ elementen globaal n▮ te zetten, evenals h▮ achtergrondperspec▮

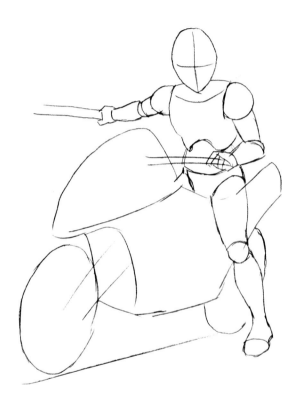

ce the bike on the
ound plane to study
proper
eshortening in this
rspective. Then draw
e figure riding the
e.

Platziere das Motorrad
auf dem Boden und
achte dabei genau auf
die Perspektive.
Zeichne anschließend
die Figur auf dem
Motorrad.

Placez la moto sur le
plan du sol afin de voir
comment la rétrécir
dans sa perspective.
Ensuite, dessinez le
personnage à cheval
sur la moto.

Plaats de motor op het
grondvlak om te
bekijken hoe hij in dit
perspectief moet
worden verkort. Teken
dan de motorrijder.

Anatomy_Anatomie_Anatomie_Anatomie

Focus on the placement of the legs and the hips, with the figure leaning and adapting to the position of the bike.

Konzentriere dich auf die Position der Beine und Hüften der nach vorne gelehnten und an das Fahrzeug geschmiegten Figur.

Concentrez-vous sur la mise en place des jambes et des hanches, avec la figure en position penchée et adaptée à celle de la moto.

Concentreer je op de plaatsing van de benen en heupen van de leunende figuur, die zich aanpast aan de positie van de motor.

e helmet has an
gular, aggressive
sign and his costume
made of a quilted
aterial that protects
s body.

Der Helm hat ein
eckiges, aggressives
Design, während der
Anzug aus einem
wattierten, den Körper
schützenden Material
besteht.

Le casque présente des
lignes anguleuses et
agressives, et le
costume est taillé dans
un tissu matelassé qui
protège le corps.

De helm heeft een
hoekig, agressief
ontwerp en het
kostuum is gemaakt
van een gevoerd
materiaal dat het
lichaam beschermt.

Lighting_Licht_Éclairage_Licht

His costume is dark, so draw shadows with big spots. Shiny areas drawn as reflections of light create a polished-metal effect.

Auf dem dunklen Anzug des Fahrers befinden sich großflächige Schatten. Die glänzenden, Licht reflektierenden Stellen hingegen erzeugen den Effekt polierten Metalls.

Le costume est sombre, il faut donc dessiner des ombres avec de larges taches de lumière. Des zones brillantes, tels des reflets lumineux, créeront un effet métallisé.

Het kostuum is donker dus teken schaduwen met grote vlekken. Glimmende delen die getekend zijn als lichtreflecties creëren het effect van gepolijst metaal.

se bright colors and
aw the sword's
ecial effect, coloring
e line and
rrounding its contour
th an airbrush-like
ine.

Verwende leuchtende
Farben und zeichne
den Spezialeffekt des
Schwertes, indem du
die Umrisslinie farbig
gestaltest und mit
einem Airbrush-
ähnlichen Schein
umgibst.

Utilisez des couleurs
éclatantes et dessinez
l'effet spécial de l'épée
en coloriant la ligne et
en en cernant les
contours au vernis
brillant type
aérographe.

Gebruik felle kleuren en
teken het speciale
effect van het zwaard
door de lijn te kleuren
en de contour ervan te
omgeven met een
airbrushachtige glans.

GANGSTER

panese gangsters, or *yakuza*, form criminal
ganizations heavily dependent on seniority
id inspired by military structure. They
>mbine Japanese business sense and
spect for tradition with the use of violence
id modern technology. You can find *yakuza*
embers with tattooed bodies and armed
th *katanas* alongside biker thugs dressed in
endy fashion.

Japanische Gangster oder Yakuza bilden
kriminelle Organisationen, die stark
hierarchisiert sind und sich an militärischen
Strukturen orientieren. Sie vereinen
japanischen Geschäftssinn und Respekt vor
der Tradition mit Gewalt und modernen
Technologien. Man findet mit Tätowierungen
übersäte oder als Katana-Kämpfer
auftretende ebenso wie elegant gekleidete
Yakuzas.

es gangsters japonais, ou yakuza, forment
es organisations criminelles extrêmement
érarchisées, à la manière des structures
ilitaires, qui allient le sens des affaires
opon, le respect de la tradition et le
cours à la violence et à la technologie
oderne. Il y a des yakusa tatoués de la tête
x pieds, qui portent encore la *katana*, mais
ssi des voyous motorisés vêtus à la
ernière mode.

Japanse gangsters of *yakuza* vormen
misdaadorganisaties met een strikte
hiërarchie en militaire structuur. Ze
combineren Japans zakeninstinct en respect
voor traditie met het gebruik van geweld en
moderne technologie. Yakuza-leden zie je
met getatoeëerde lichamen en gewapend
met katana's naast trendy geklede zware
jongens op motoren.

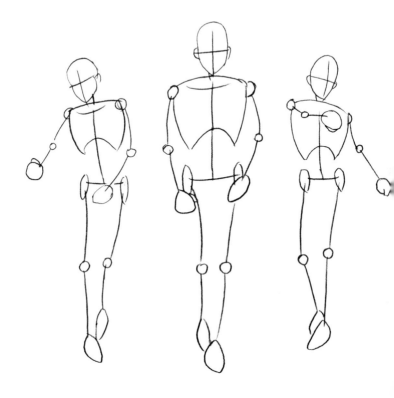

In this ensemble, be very careful to balance the space allotted in front of and between the three figures.

Achte bei dieser Gruppe besonders auf die Ausgewogenheit des Raums vor und zwischen den Figuren.

Pour ce groupe, prenez bien soin d'équilibrer l'espace disponible devant et entre les trois personnages.

Zoek in dit ensemble heel zorgvuldig de balans in de ruimte voor en tussen de drie figuren.

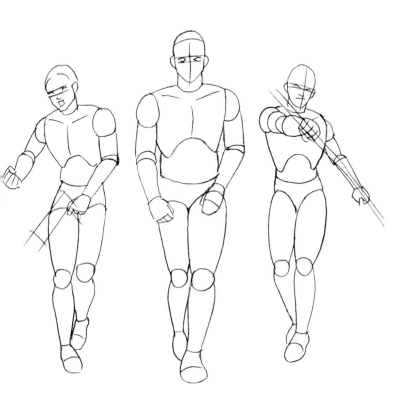

e a standard
rspective here, with
y normal
portions and few
eshortenings.

Verwende eine
Standardperspektive
mit normalen
Proportionen und nur
wenig Tiefe.

Utilisez ici une
perspective standard,
avec des proportions
tout à fait normales et
peu de
rétrécissements.

Gebruik hier een
standaardperspectief,
met heel normale
proporties en weinig
verkortingen.

Anatomy_Anatomie_Anatomie_Anatomie

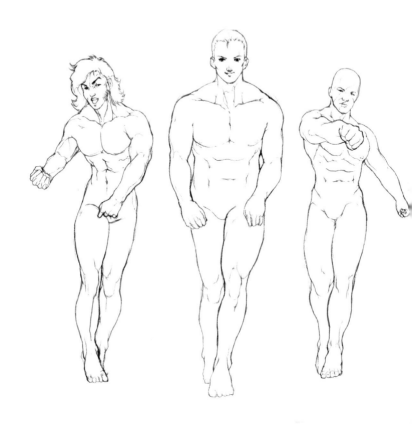

Complete the drawing, taking into account that the features and height of each character are different.

Vervollständige den Entwurf und achte dabei darauf, dass sich Merkmale und Größe einer jeden Figur unterscheiden.

Complétez le dessin, en gardant à l'esprit que chaque personnage possède une taille et des traits différents.

Voltooi de tekening; houd er rekening mee dat de gelaatstrekken en lengte van elk personage anders zijn

othing is essential in der to reflect each aracter's job; elegant thes can help stinguish their rank.

Die Kleidung spielt hier eine wichtige Rolle, da sie die Rolle ihrer Träger definiert. Elegante Kleidung zeigt einen hohen Rang an.

Les vêtements sont essentiels : ils reflètent la profession de chaque personnage ; des habits élégants peuvent aider à différencier les grades.

Aan de kleding zie je wat elk personage doet. Hoe eleganter de kleren, hoe hoger iemands plek in de hiërarchie.

Lighting_Licht_Éclairage_Licht

Use very detailed
shadow work to model
the clothes of the
different characters
and large shades to
mark the shape of the
folds.

Arbeite die Schatten
sorgfältig heraus, um
die unterschiedlichen
Kleidungsstile zu
betonen. Setze
großflächige Schatten
für die Falten ein.

Travaillez les ombres
dans le détail pour
modeler les vêtements
des différents
personnages, et utilisez
de larges dégradés
pour marquer la forme
des plis.

Gebruik heel
gedetailleerde schadu
om de kleren van de
verschillende
personages vorm te
geven. Maak grote
schaduwen voor de
vorm van de plooien.

color the figures, try
very limited range of
olors with a common
ne that pulls the
omposition together.

Verwende eine
begrenzte Farbpalette
mit einem einzigen
Grundton, um eine
harmonische
Komposition zu
erhalten.

Pour colorier les
personnages, essayez
une gamme très limitée
de couleurs, avec une
teinte commune pour
unifier la composition.

Kleur de figuren met
behulp van een heel
beperkt palet met een
gemeenschappelijke
tint die de compositie
tot een eenheid maakt.

PY

ofessional assassin-spies are specially
ined in martial arts, weapons and
ltration. They have to be sharp, agile and
e to improvise in complex situations. To
d some sex appeal to our design, we have
osen to draw a girl and have opted for a
s violent design. We will substitute the
ual weapons for an action pose on a
toon background.

Professionelle Killer-Spione besitzen
besondere Kenntnisse in Kampfsportarten,
Waffen und Einbruchtechniken. Sie müssen
flink und beweglich sein und die Fähigkeit
besitzen, in schwierigen Situationen schnell
zu reagieren. Um unserer Zeichnung ein
wenig Sex-Apppeal zu verleihen, zeichnen wir
ein Mädchen und verwenden ein nicht allzu
aggressives Design. Die kampflustige
Körperhaltung vor einem Comic-Hintergrund
ersetzt die normalerweise gezeigten Waffen.

s espions meurtriers professionnels sont
écialement entraînés aux arts martiaux, au
niement des armes et aux techniques
nfiltration. Ils doivent avoir l'esprit aigu et
et être capables d'improviser dans les
uations compliquées. Pour ajouter un rien
sex-appeal à notre portrait, nous avons
oisi de dessiner une fille et de miser sur
style moins violent. Nous remplacerons
armes habituelles par une attitude
rtiale sur fond de bande dessinée.

Professionele spionnen/huurmoordenaars
zijn speciaal getraind in vechtsporten,
wapengebruik en infiltratie. Ze moeten
scherp en behendig zijn en in staat zijn te
improviseren in ingewikkelde situaties. Om
de tekening wat sexappeal te geven, hebben
we gekozen voor een meisje en een minder
gewelddadig ontwerp. In plaats van de
gebruikelijke wapens tekenen we een
actiepose tegen een strip-achtergrond.

Shape_Form_Forme_Vorm

Focus on the line of motion, and begin by sketching the foreshortened limbs with the feet positioned firmly on the ground.

Achte besonders auf die Bewegungslinie – beginne mit der perspektivischen Zeichnung der Beine, die Füße stehen fest auf dem Boden.

Concentrez-vous sur la ligne de mouvement, et commencez par esquisser les membres rétrécis, avec les pieds fermement positionnés au sol.

Concentreer je op de bewegingslijn en schets eerst de verkorte ledematen met de voeten stevig op de grond.

ish the
eshortened
ments, focusing on
e arms. It's best to
st fit in the torso and
en add the other
ments.

Konzentriere dich
anschließend auf die
Arme, beginne beim
Oberkörper und füge
dann die anderen
Elemente hinzu.

Terminez les éléments
rétrécis, en vous
concentrant sur les
bras. Il vaut mieux
d'abord mettre en
place le torse, puis
ajouter les autres
éléments.

Voltooi de verkorte
elementen; concentreer
je op de armen. Je kunt
het beste eerst de
romp inpassen en dan
de andere elementen
toevoegen.

Anatomy_Anatomie_Anatomie_Anatomie

This character is slim and elegant but at the same time quite robust and athletic. Her anatomy must look strong, not muscular.

Die Figur dieser Agentin ist schlank und elegant, aber gleichzeitig robust und athletisch – ihre Anatomie wirkt kräftig, aber nicht muskulös.

Ce personnage est mince et élégant, mais également robuste et athlétique. Son anatomie doit produire une impression de force, pas de musculature.

Dit personage is slank en elegant, maar ook vrij robuust en atletisch. De anatomi moet er niet gespierd maar wel sterk uitzier

he is an elite agent uipped with the test weapons and ectronic gadgets. The arf around her neck nds a feminine touch.

Als Eliteagentin ist sie mit modernsten Waffen und Hightech-Geräten ausgestattet. Durch den Schal verleihst du ihr einen femininen Touch.

Il s'agit d'un agent d'élite, équipé d'armes et de gadgets électroniques dernier cri. L'écharpe autour de son cou fournit la touche féminine.

Zij is een eliteagent met de nieuwste wapens en elektronische snufjes. De sjaal om haar nek zorgt voor een vrouwelijke noot.

Lighting_Licht_Éclairage_Licht

Using overhead light, shadows mold the volume of her sinuous shape. Contrasting tonalities helps differentiate elements.

Das von oben einfallende Licht unterstreicht ihre geschmeidige Figur, wobei kontrastreiche Schattierungen dazu dienen, die einzelnen Elemente voneinander abzugrenzen.

Avec une lumière venant d'en haut, les ombres modèlent le volume de ses formes ondoyantes. Des tonalités contrastées aideront à différencier les éléments.

Met licht van bovenaf modelleren schaduwe het volume van de welvingen. Door tonaliteiten te laten contrasteren, kun je onderscheid aanbrengen tussen elementen

Contrast marks this design's chromatic range. Combine the sobriety of the gray with the strength and luminosity of the reds.

Die Farbskala zeichnet sich durch starke Kontraste aus: Kombiniere nüchternes Grau mit leuchtenden Rottönen.

Le contraste caractérise ici l'éventail chromatique. Combinez la sobriété du gris avec la force et la luminosité des rouges.

Contrast kenmerkt het palet van dit ontwerp. Combineer het ingetogen grijs met krachtige, stralende roodtinten.

LAKE MONSTER

these forgotten lands, even relaxing by the dge of a lake can be dangerous. Before men nd *orcs* existed, when the earth was overed with water, these monsters already ved all over the world, preying on anything ithin reach. Sometimes playful, sometimes oracious, they don't think twice about ctacking those foolish enough to get near e water.

In dieser vergessenen Welt kann es sogar gefährlich sein, sich an einem Seeufer aufzuhalten. Vor der Existenz von Menschen und Orks war die Erde von Wasser bedeckt – diese Seeungeheuer besiedelten zu dieser Zeit bereits die Erde und jagten alles, was in ihre Nähe kam. Sie greifen jeden an, der sich nahe genug ans Wasser traut, sei es aus purer Angriffslust oder weil der Hunger sie treibt.

ans ces contrées oubliées, tout est angereux, même prendre un peu de repos bord d'un lac. Avant la naissance des ommes et des orques, lorsque la terre était uverte d'eau, ces monstres peuplaient déjà monde, faisant leur proie de tout ce dont pouvaient s'emparer. Parfois joueurs, arfois voraces, ils n'y regardent pas à deux is avant d'attaquer quiconque est assez fou our s'approcher de l'eau.

In dit vergeten rijk kan het zelfs gevaarlijk zijn om uit te rusten aan de rand van een meer. Voordat er mensen en orks bestonden, toen de aarde bedekt was met water, bevolkten deze monsters al de hele wereld en joegen ze op alles wat ze zagen. Deze soms speelse, soms verscheurende wezens vallen zonder aarzelen mensen aan die dwaas genoeg zijn om in de buurt van het water te komen.

Shape_Form_Forme_Vorm

Create a point of connection between the two characters.	Stelle eine optische Verbindung zwischen den beiden Charakteren her.	Créez un point de connexion entre les deux personnages.	Creëer een verbinding punt tussen de twee personages.

The volumes will be malleable, not solid. Avoid straight lines.	Die Volumen sind beweglich und biegsam, verhindere daher gerade Linien.	Les volumes seront malléables, pas solides. Évitez les lignes droites.	De volumes moeten een plooibaar karakter hebben, dus gebruik geen rechte lijnen.

Anatomy_Anatomie_Anatomie_Anatomie

The warrior is strong and able to withstand the monster's attacks. The creature is aggressive, so make its muscles look tense.

Der Krieger zeichnet sich durch Stärke und Mut aus, so kann er den Angriffen des Ungeheuers, dessen angespannte Muskeln sichtbar sind, widerstehen.

Le guerrier est robuste et capable de résister aux assauts du monstre. La créature est agressive, faites en sorte que ses muscles aient l'air tendus.

De strijder is sterk en weerstaat de aanvaller van het monster. Omdat het beest agressief is, moeten zijn spieren er gespannen uitzien.

Avoid overdressing the warrior so we don't take attention away from the main figure.

Um den Fokus auf das Seeungeheuer zu richten, wird der Krieger mit nur wenig Kleidung und Attributen ausgestattet.

Évitez de trop vêtir le guerrier afin de ne pas détourner l'attention du personnage principal.

Kleed de strijder niet te opvallend, anders leidt hij de aandacht af van de hoofdfiguur.

Lighting_Licht_Éclairage_Licht

Use contrasting shadows that come from a single source of light.

Setze kontrastreiche Schatten ein, die durch eine einzige Lichtquelle produziert werden.

Utilisez des ombres contrastées venant d'une seule source de lumière.

Gebruik contrasterend schaduwen die worden veroorzaakt door één lichtbron.

aint the scales one-
y-one, creating volume
y coloring some in a
ase color, others in
ther a darker color or
lighter one.

Zeichne die Schuppen
einzeln nacheinander
und gib der Figur
Volumen, indem du
einige der Schuppen in
Basisfarben, andere
dunkler oder heller
einfärbst.

Peignez les écailles une
à une, et créez du
volume en en coloriant
certaines de la couleur
du support, d'autres
dans une teinte plus
foncée ou plus claire.

Kleur de schubben één
voor één; creëer
volume door sommige
een grondkleur te
geven en andere een
donkere of lichtere
kleur.

NINJA

During the Japanese Middle Ages, a turbulent period, it was necessary to organize a force of spies and mercenaries. The feudal lords used these agents, trained to infiltrate and kill, in a civil war that affected a great many small owners. With the unification of Japan, and the arrival of modern times, ninja stories became legend and *ninjitsu* became a sport.

Im turbulenten japanischen Mittelalter existierten zahlreiche aus Spionen und Söldnern bestehende Streitmächte. Die von den Feudalherren eingesetzten Agenten waren darauf trainiert, sich an bestimmten Orten einzuschmuggeln und zu töten. Dieser „Bürgerkrieg" kostete zahllose kleine Landbesitzer das Leben. Mit der Vereinigung Japans und dem Anbruch des modernen Zeitalters wurden die Ninja-Geschichten zur Legende und Ninjitsu zu einer Sportart.

Au Japon, durant l'époque troublée du Moyen-Âge, il fallut organiser une force d'espions et de mercenaires. Les seigneurs féodaux utilisèrent ces agents, passés maîtres dans l'art d'infiltrer et de tuer, lors d'une guerre civile dont furent victimes un grand nombre de petits propriétaires. Avec l'unification du Japon et l'arrivée des temps modernes, les récits de *ninjas* sont devenus des légendes, et le *ninjitsu* est aujourd'hui une discipline sportive.

Tijdens de turbulente Japanse middeleeuwen was het noodzakelijk om een macht van spionnen en huurlingen te organiseren. De feodale heren gebruikten deze mensen, die getraind werden om te infiltreren en te doden, in een burgeroorlog die veel kleine bezitters trof. Met de eenwording van Japan en het aanbreken van de moderne tijd werden ninjaverhalen legendes en werd ninjitsu een sport.

Shape_Form_Forme_Vorm

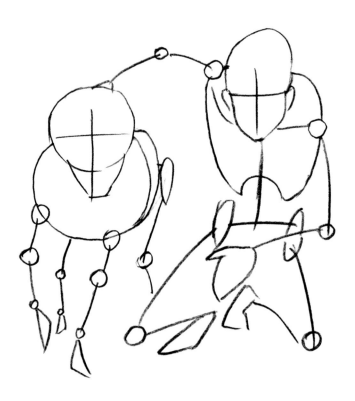

Sketch the image of a dog in an alert position. The *ninja* is crouching and passes an arm over the animal's back.

Skizziere einen Hund in wachsamer Haltung. Der Ninja kniet neben ihm, seine Hand ruht auf dem Rücken des Tiers.

Dessinez la forme d'un chien à l'arrêt. Le *ninja* est accroupi, un bras passé autour de l'échine du chien.

Schets een hond in ee waakzame houding. D ninja kruipt en legt zij arm over de rug van h dier.

how the volume of the gures from a slightly w angle, such as hen drawing the wolf- og's back and legs.

Zeichne die Figuren aus einer leichten Froschperspektive heraus, besonders fällt dies beim Rücken und den Beinen des Hundes auf.

Montrez le volume des silhouettes en légère contre-plongée, notamment en dessinant l'échine et les pattes du chien- loup.

Toon het volume van de figuren vanuit een ietwat laag perspectief, bijvoorbeeld wanneer je de rug en poten van de wolf-hond tekent.

Anatomy_Anatomie_Anatomie_Anatomie

The *ninja* is resting on his knees in front of us; therefore, the legs are hidden behind the upper part of the legs and the knees.

Die Unterschenkel des vor uns knienden Ninja befinden sich unter seinen Oberschenkeln und Knien.

Le *ninja* repose sur ses genoux et nous fait face ; la partie inférieure de ses jambes est donc cachée par les cuisses et les genoux.

De ninja rust op zijn knieën voor ons; de onderbenen gaan daarom schuil achter de bovenbenen en de knieën.

ake sure to adhere to
e stereotype; while
etails can change, the
ose garments, masks
d wristbands are
oligatory.

Wichtig ist es, den
Ninja mit den typischen
Merkmalen wie einem
flatternden Gewand,
Masken und
Armbändern
auszustatten.

Veillez à coller au
stéréotype ; si les
détails peuvent
changer, les habits
amples, le masque et le
poignet de force, eux,
sont obligatoires.

Houd je aan de
stereotiepe kleding; de
details kunnen variëren,
maar de wijde kleding-
stukken, maskers en
polsbanden zijn onont-
beerlijk.

Lighting_Licht_Éclairage_Licht

Normally we'll design *ninja* garments to blend with the darkness. Here the artist chose light clothes and an illuminated scene.

Normalerweise tragen Ninja Gewänder, die mit der Dunkelheit verschmelzen, hier allerdings wählte der Künstler helle Kleidungsstücke und eine beleuchtete Umgebung.

En principe, on dessinera les habits du *ninja* de manière à ce qu'ils se fondent avec les ténèbres. Ici, l'artiste a choisi d'éclairer les vêtements et d'illuminer la scène.

Normaal passen we ninjakleren aan het donker aan. Hier heeft de tekenaar gekozen voor lichte kleren en een verlicht tafereel.

This *ninja* may be on a mission in a region with a lot of snow. The colors complement the pale gray of the wolf-dog's coat.

Der Ninja könnte auf einer Mission durch ein schneereiches Gebiet unterwegs sein. Das helle Grau des Hundefells harmoniert perfekt mit den restlichen Farben.

Ce *ninja* pourrait être en mission dans une contrée très enneigée. Les couleurs complètent le gris pale de la robe du chien-loup.

Deze ninja is wellicht op een missie in een gebied met veel sneeuw. De kleuren vullen het bleke grijs van de vacht van de wolf-hond aan.

MEDUSA

Medusa is an ancient Greek mythological creature with the body of a woman from head to hips, and of a snake hips downward. Her hair is also a frightening mass of snakes. Medusa was a dangerous archer, who poisoned the arrows she used with her own saliva. But she had an even more terrible power: transforming anyone who looked directly at her eyes into stone.

Medusa ist eine Figur aus der griechischen Mythologie. Vom Kopf bis zu den Hüften besitzt sie den Körper einer Frau, ihre Beine haben Schlangengestalt, ihr Haar besteht aus Furcht erregenden Schlangen. Als gefährliche Bogenschützin präparierte sie ihre todbringenden Pfeile mit ihrem eigenen giftigen Speichel. Medusa besaß allerdings eine noch fürchterlichere Fähigkeit: Sie ließ jeden, der ihr in die Augen sah, zu Stein erstarren.

La méduse est une ancienne créature de la mythologie grecque, avec un corps de femme de la tête aux hanches, puis de serpent à partir de la ceinture. Sa chevelure est une effrayante masse de serpents entremêlés. La méduse est un dangereux archer, qui empoisonne les flèches qu'elle utilise avec sa propre salive. Mais elle possède un pouvoir encore plus terrible : celui de changer en pierre quiconque la regarde dans les yeux.

Medusa is een oud-Grieks mythologisch wezen met van hoofd tot heupen het lichaam van een vrouw en vanaf de heupen dat van een slang. Het haar is ook een ijzingwekkende kluwen slangen. Medusa was een gevaarlijke boogschutter die de pijlen met haar eigen speeksel van gif voorzag. Maar nog huiveringwekkender was haar vermogen om iedereen die direct in haar ogen keek in steen te veranderen.

Shape_Form_Forme_Vorm

Sketch a human figure, but instead of legs, make a continuous line. Prolong the vertical axis following the curve of the back.

Zeichne einen menschlichen Körper, die Beine bestehen jedoch aus einer gebogenen Linie. Verlängere dabei die vertikale Achse des Rückens.

Esquissez une figure humaine en traçant, à la place des jambes, une ligne continue. Prolongez l'axe vertical en suivant la courbe du dos.

Schets een menselijke figuur, maar teken in plaats van benen een doorlopende lijn. Trek de verticale as door; volg daarbij de welving van de rug.

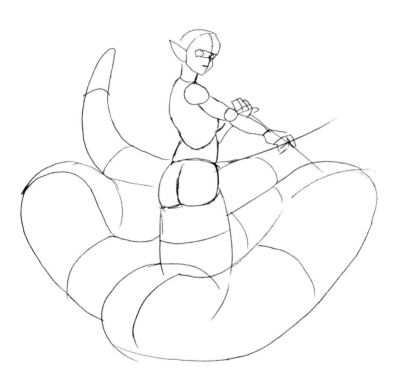

Draw the upper body normally. Below, draw the body of the snake; it should be coiled up so it fits completely within the frame.

Gib dem Oberkörper eine ganz normale menschliche Gestalt, der nach unten hin in einen zusammengerollten Schlangenkörper übergeht und genau in den Rahmen passt.

Dessinez la partie supérieure du corps normalement. En dessous, dessinez le corps d'un serpent ; il doit être enroulé sur lui-même pour pouvoir tenir dans le cadre.

Teken het bovenlichaam normaal. Teken van onderen een slangenlijf, dat opgerold moet zijn zodat het helemaal binnen het kader past.

Anatomy_Anatomie_Anatomie_Anatomie

The body of the snake is soft. So when it coils, it creates folds. Draw where the snakes on her head pass and overlap.

Aufgrund seiner weichen Oberfläche bildet der zusammengerollte Schlangenkörper Falten. Deute die sich umschlingenden Schlangen auf dem Kopf an.

Le corps du serpent est souple. Quand il s'enroule, des plis se forment. Dessinez l'endroit où les serpents se mêlent et se chevauchent sur sa tête.

Het lichaam van de slang is zacht. Er ontstaan dus plooien als het zich oprolt. Gee' aan waar de slangen op het hoofd van Medusa elkaar overlappen.

is important to
elineate the figure's
olume and the snake's
ody: shadows help to
now the overlapping of
e folds.

Grenze mithilfe des
Schattenwurfs den
menschlichen und den
schlangenähnlichen Teil
des Körpers
voneinander ab.

Il est important de
délinéer le volume de la
silhouette et le corps
du serpent ; les ombres
contribuent à montrer
la superposition des
plis.

Het is belangrijk om het
volume van de figuur en
het slangenlijf duidelijk
weer te geven; met
schaduw toon je het
overlappen van de
plooien.

Color_Farben_Couleur_Kleur

Apply a solid-color base to highlight certain areas. Then clarify with shading and add textural effects to the snake's skin.

Trage zunächst eine deckende Farbschicht auf, um bestimmte Bereiche zu betonen. Füge anschließend die Schattierungen und Oberflächenstrukturen der Schlangenhaut hinzu.

Appliquez une base opaque pour mettre en valeur certaines zones. Ensuite, éclaircissez en nuançant et ajoutez des effets de texture à la peau du serpent.

Breng een basis in één kleur aan om bepaalde delen te accentueren. Nuanceer het geheel met schaduw en voeg textuureffecten toe aan de slangenhuid.

nally, add the back
nage, a classical
osaic that suits the
naracter and gives a
etter ambiance to the
cene.

Runde die Zeichnung
anschließend mit einem
klassischen, zur Figur
passenden Mosaikbild
im Hintergrund ab, um
der Szene Atmosphäre
zu verleihen.

Pour finir, ajoutez
l'arrière-plan : une
mosaïque classique
assortie au personnage,
qui confère à la scène
davantage
d'atmosphère.

Voeg ten slotte de
achtergrond toe, een
klassiek mozaïek dat
past bij het personage
en het tafereel een
betere sfeer geeft.

SORCERER

A sorcerer is a king of wizards or magicians who deals with dark creatures and offers them bloody sacrifices in exchange for supernatural powers and immortality. We are going to draw an Asian sorcerer who, in trying to mock death, has become transformed into a kind of ghost. This terrifying creature needs to consume the body of a young girl for his reincarnation.

Ein Hexenmeister ist der Herrscher über Zauberer oder Magier, der mit dunklen Kreaturen verkehrt. Diesen verspricht er blutige Opfer, um übernatürliche Kräfte und Unsterblichkeit zu erlangen. Hier soll ein asiatischer Hexenmeister dargestellt werden, der sich, um den Tod zu überlisten, in eine Art Geist verwandelt hat. Für seine Wiedergeburt benötigt dieses fürchterliche Wesen den Körper eines jungen Mädchens.

Une sorcière est une sorte de magicienne ou enchanteur qui commerce avec les créatures des ténèbres et leur offre des sacrifices sanglants en échange de pouvoirs surnaturels et de l'immortalité. Nous allons dessiner une sorcière asiatique qui, cherchant à tromper la mort, s'est transformée en une sorte de spectre. Cette créature terrifiante doit consommer le corps d'une jeune fille pour pouvoir se réincarner.

Een tovenaar is een koning van magiërs die zich inlaat met duistere wezens, aan wie hij bloederige offers brengt in ruil voor bovenatuurlijke krachten en onsterfelijkheid. We tekenen een Aziatische tovenaar die veranderd is in een soort geest om de spot te drijven met de dood. Dit huiveringwekkende wezen moet het lichaam van een jong meisje verslinden om een menselijke vorm aan te nemen.

Sketch the different parts of the body: the head, the torso and the arms.

Skizziere die verschiedenen Körperteile: Kopf, Oberkörper und Arme.

Esquissez les différentes parties du corps : la tête, le torse et les bras.

Schets de diverse lichaamsdelen: het hoofd, de romp en de armen.

The foreshortening of the hand is very pronounced and gives the image a lot of movement.

Die nach vorne ausgestreckte Hand befindet sich im Vordergrund des Bildes und verleiht diesem Bewegung.

Le rétrécissement de la main, très prononcé, donne à l'image beaucoup de mouvement.

Doordat de hand sterk verkort is, krijgt de afbeelding veel beweging.

Clothes_Kleidung_Vêtements_Kleren

Seek references of *kimonos* and similar costumes and draw a simple sketch to control the shape and achieve a sense of motion.

Nimm die Abbildungen von Kimonos und ähnlichen Kleidungsstücken als Vorbild und zeichne zunächst eine einfache Skizze, um seine Form und den Bewegungsfluss zu erfassen.

Cherchez des références de kimonos et de costumes analogues, puis faites une simple esquisse pour en maîtriser la forme et leur donner du mouvement.

Zoek afbeeldingen van kimono's en vergelijkbare kledingstukken en maak een eenvoudige schets om de vorm te leren beheersen en een zekere dynamiek te kunnen creëren.

The background light is supernatural. Highlight features by mixing xpressionist effects with the different light nd contrasts.

Der Hintergrund ist mit einem magischen Licht erfüllt. Betone einzelne Bereiche, indem du expressionistisch wirkende Effekte mit verschiedenen Lichteffekten und Kontrasten kombinierst.

La lumière de l'arrière-plan est surnaturelle. Mettez en valeur les traits en associant des effets expressionnistes avec les différents éclairages et contrastes.

Het achtergrondlicht is bovennatuurlijk. Breng accenten aan door expressionistische effecten te combineren met de diverse lichten en contrasten.

Color_Farben_Couleur_Kleur

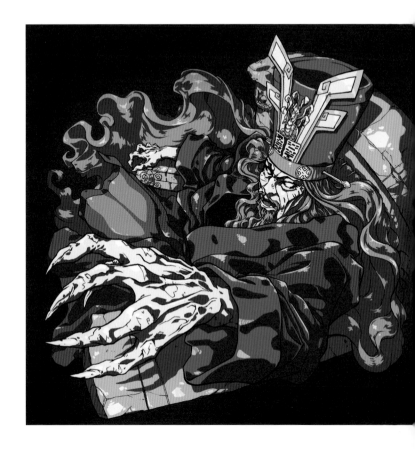

Color the figure and, at the same time, sketch the folds and shadows of the costume. Use intense, saturated colors.

Betone beim Einfärben der Figur gleichzeitig die Falten und Schatten der Kleidung, verwende dabei gesättigte Farbtöne.

Coloriez le personnage et, en même temps, ébauchez les plis et les ombres du costume. Utilisez des couleurs intenses et saturées.

Kleur de figuur en schets tegelijkertijd de plooien en schaduwen van het kostuum. Gebruik intense, verzadigde kleuren.

Draw a face with Asian features, such as a long moustache and an elaborate hairstyle, as well as long fingernails.

Zeichne ein asiatisch wirkendes Gesicht mit einem langen Bart, flatternden Haaren und spitzen, langen Fingernägeln.

Dessinez un visage aux traits asiatiques, ainsi qu'une longue moustache et une coiffure élaborée, et de très longs ongles.

Teken een gezicht met Aziatische trekken. Geef het bijvoorbeeld een lange snor en een complex kapsel. Teken ook lange vingernagels.

ORC

This vile and inhuman race is not very attractive or intelligent. However, his muscular physique and crazed look make him truly terrifying and unpredictable. We will draw him in a natural environment, half crouching and about to throw himself upon his prey. The weapons he uses are very rudimentary. Making them hardly involves more than smelting down the metal.

Dieses abscheuliche, unmenschliche Wesen ist hässlich und von geringer Intelligenz. Durch eine muskulöse Gestalt und sein absonderliches Aussehen wirkt es fürchterlich und unberechenbar. Wir platzieren diesen Ork in eine natürliche Umgebung, in halb hockender Position und jederzeit bereit, über seine Beute herzufallen. Seine Waffen sind äußerst primitiv und bestehen selten aus geschmiedetem Metall.

Cette race vile et inhumaine n'est ni très séduisante ni très intelligente. Toutefois, sa musculature et son allure démente la rendent vraiment terrifiante et imprévisible. Nous dessinerons ce personnage dans un environnement naturel, mi-accroupi et sur le point de s'abattre sur sa proie. Les armes qu'il utilise sont très rudimentaires. Leur fabrication ne demande guère d'autres aptitudes que de savoir fondre le métal.

Dit weerzinwekkende en onmenselijke ras is niet erg aantrekkelijk of intelligent. Met hun gespierde lijf en waanzinnige blik zien orks er angstaanjagend en onvoorspelbaar uit. We tekenen deze ork in een natuurlijke omgeving; hij staat op het punt zijn prooi te bespringen. Zijn wapens zijn heel basaal: de vervaardiging ervan vergt nauwelijks meer dan het smelten van het metaal.

Shape_Form_Forme_Vorm

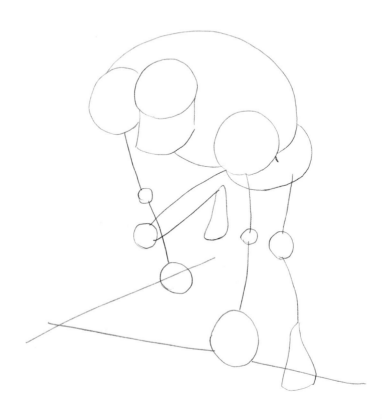

Crouching; extremities and body very close.

Durch die kniende Position befinden sich Körper und Gliedmaße nahe beieinander.

Accroupie ; extrémités et corps ramassés.

Voorovergebogen; ledematen en romp dicht bij elkaar.

He is a heavily built character, with a large, rectangular jaw. Draw a broad back and robust arms and legs.

Seine Figur ist grobschlächtig: der Kiefer riesig und eckig, der Rücken breit, Arme und Beine kräftig.

Il s'agit d'un personnage très charpenté, avec une large mâchoire rectangulaire. Dessinez un large dos, ainsi que des bras et des jambes robustes.

De ork is extreem zwaargebouwd en heeft grote, rechthoekige kaken. Teken een brede rug en robuuste armen en benen.

Anatomy_Anatomie_Anatomie_Anatomie

Unequal eyes increase his crazed expression. Veins emphasize tension in a face that says "I've got no friends".

Unterschiedliche Augen und hervortretende Adern betonen seine Absonderlichkeit, das angespannte Gesicht drückt aus: „Ich habe keine Freunde".

Des yeux de taille inégale auront pour effet de renforcer l'expression démente. Des nervures soulignent la tension d'un visage qui dit "Je n'ai aucun ami".

Het verschil tussen de ogen versterkt de waanzinnige gelaatsuitdrukking. De aders benadrukken de spanning in een gezicht dat zegt: "Ik heb geen vrienden."

he leather straps,
hackles, chains and
iercings give him a
nacabre appearance.
pinal blades reinforce
he punk style.

Lederriemen, Ketten
und Piercings sorgen
für ein grausiges
Erscheinungsbild, die
Stacheln auf dem
Rücken wirken wie eine
Punkfrisur.

Les sangles de cuir, les
anneaux métalliques,
les chaînes et le
piercing donnent au
personnage son
apparence macabre.
L'épine dorsale de
saurien renforce le
style punk.

De leren riemen,
boeien, kettingen en
piercings geven hem
een macaber
voorkomen. De
kammen op zijn rug
versterken de punkstijl.

Lightly reinforce the silhouette's outline. Project the shadow onto the ground.

Verstärke dezent die Umrisslinie der Gestalt und zeichne den Schattenwurf auf den Boden.

Renforcez légèrement les contours de la silhouette. Projetez l'ombre sur le sol.

Zet het silhouet wat meer aan. Teken de schaduw die de ork op de grond werpt.

Color the illustration with different shades of green and apply various tones to highlight small details and avoid confusion.

Verwende verschiedene Grüntöne und betone mit unterschiedlichen Schattierungen kleine Details, achte jedoch darauf, dich nicht zu verzetteln.

Coloriez l'image avec différentes nuances de vert et appliquez plusieurs teintes pour mettre en valeur les petits détails et éviter la confusion.

Kleur de afbeelding met verschillende tinten groen en breng diverse kleurnuances aan om kleine details te accentueren en verwarring te vermijden.

EVIL GODDESS

he Evil Goddess is a deity capable of using
er will to bring her desires to life. Her
omains exist in a different dimension and
he usually has demon servants to help her
onquer the world of the mortals. We are
oing to draw a goddess who does not reveal
er real form; rather she appears in the
easing form that her mortal vassals
ecognize.

Die Göttin des Bösen besitzt genug Macht,
um sich alle ihre Begehren zu erfüllen. Ihr
Reich erstreckt sich über verschiedenen
Dimensionen, und Dämonen stehen ihr bei
der Eroberung der Menschenwelt zur Seite.
Unsere Göttin gibt ihre wahre Gestalt nicht
preis, sondern erscheint in der attraktiven
Gestalt einer Sterblichen.

a Déesse du Mal est une divinité capable
'utiliser ses pouvoirs pour réaliser ses
ésirs. Ses domaines s'étendent à plusieurs
imensions et elle a généralement pour
erviteurs des démons qui l'aident à
onquérir le monde des mortels. Nous allons
essiner une déesse qui ne révèle pas sa
éritable forme ; elle préfère se montrer sous
apparence agréable que connaissent ses
ortels vassaux.

De Godin van het Kwaad is een godheid die
door middel van haar wil haar verlangens tot
leven kan brengen. Haar rijk is in een andere
dimensie en meestal heeft ze demonische
dienaren die haar de wereld van de
stervelingen helpen veroveren. Wij gaan een
godin tekenen die niet haar ware vorm
prijsgeeft, maar de bevallige gedaante
aanneemt die haar sterfelijke knechten
herkennen.

Shape_Form_Forme_Vorm

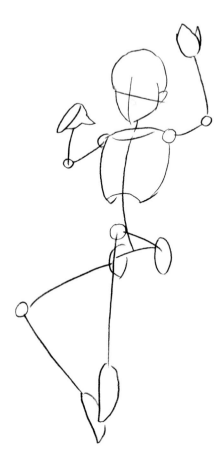

Draw the figure of the character leaning on the sword by sketching a straight line referencing the position of the sword.

Zeichne die Figur auf einem Schwert lehnend und stelle dir dabei das Schwert als eine gerade Linie vor.

Dessinez la silhouette du personnage appuyée contre l'épée, en traçant une ligne droite pour marquer l'emplacement de l'arme.

Geef met een rechte lijn de positie weer van het zwaard waarop het personage leunt.

Make a complete sketch of the figure of the Evil Goddess and give shape to the sword.

Vervollständige die Skizze und zeichne nun auch das Schwert ein.

Faites une esquisse complète de la figure de la Déesse du Mal, et donnez forme à l'épée.

Maak een volledige schets van de godin en geef het zwaard vorm.

Anatomy_Anatomie_Anatomie_Anatomie

Soften the line of her contour so her flesh appears soft. Be careful to draw the folds around certain parts of her body properly.

Gestalte die Umrisslinie mit weichen Rändern, um ihre Haut zart erscheinen zu lassen. Achte dabei besonders auf die Hautfalten an bestimmten Körperstellen.

Atténuez les contours afin que la chair paraisse douce. Dessinez très soigneusement les plis autour de certaines parties du corps.

Maak de lijn van haar contour zachter, zodat het vlees ook zachter lijkt. Zorg ervoor dat je de plooien rondom bepaalde delen van haar lichaam correct tekent.

Abundant, long hair helps give the goddess presence. Play with shadows so the contours of the figures merge with one another.

Langes wehendes Haar sorgt für ein beeindruckendes Erscheinungsbild. Spiele mit den Schatten, sodass die Konturen der Figur miteinander verschmelzen.

Une longue et épaisse chevelure contribue à donner de la présence à la déesse. Jouez des ombres afin que les contours des silhouettes se fondent entre eux.

Lang, weelderig haar versterkt de aanwezigheid van de godin. Speel met schaduwen, zodat de contouren van de figuren in elkaar overlopen.

Lighting_Licht_Éclairage_Licht

The lighting highlights the deep shades in the background. Amplify the evil atmosphere by creating a sense of darkness.

Durch Beleuchtung werden die tiefen Schatten im Hintergrund hervorgehoben, verstärke diese teuflische Atmosphäre durch einen dunklen Hintergrund.

L'éclairage met en valeur les nuances appuyées de l'arrière-plan. Amplifiez l'atmosphère satanique en créant une sensation de ténèbres.

Het licht accentueert de donkere schaduwen op de achtergrond. Versterk de boosaardige sfeer door een gevoel van duisternis te creëren.

As you can see, it is easy to associate absolute evil with dark tones. Note the predominance of black and blue shadings.

Wie du siehst, lässt sich das Böse ganz einfach mit dunklen Farben darstellen. Beachte besonders die Dominanz schwarzer und blauer Farbtöne.

Comme vous le voyez, il est aisé d'associer le mal absolu avec les tons sombres. Notez la prédominance des nuances de noir et de bleu.

Zoals je ziet, kun je absoluut kwaad goed weergeven met donkere tinten. Zwarte en blauwe schakeringen overheersen.

MUMMY

The origin of mummies goes back to ancient Egypt, which had the custom of embalming and mummifying important people. They are often accompanied by pyramids, excavations and archaeological relics. Since they tend to be a bit clumsy when walking, they sometimes start losing bandages and even parts of their bodies, due to their gradual but constant deterioration.

Mumien stammen ursprünglich aus dem alten Ägypten, wo bedeutende Persönlichkeiten nach ihrem Tod einbalsamiert und mumifiziert wurden. Sie befinden sich häufig in Pyramiden, umgeben von archäologischen Schätzen. Aufgrund ihrer schwerfälligen Gangart lösen sich Teile der Bandagen – der Verwesungsprozess sorgt dafür, dass sie immer wieder einzelne Körperteile verlieren.

L'origine des momies remonte à l'Égypte ancienne, où l'on avait coutume d'embaumer et de momifier les hauts personnages. Elles vont souvent de pair avec des pyramides, des fouilles et des vestiges archéologiques. Comme elles ont du mal à marcher, il arrive qu'elles perdent leurs bandelettes, voire même un membre de temps en temps, en raison de leur dégradation progressive, mais constante.

Mummies vinden hun oorsprong in het oude Egypte, waar men gewoon was om belangrijke mensen te balsemen en te mummificeren. Ze gaan vaak vergezeld van piramides, opgravingen en archeologische objecten. Doordat ze een beetje stuntelig lopen, verliezen ze soms windels en – door hun geleidelijke, maar voortdurende ontbidding – zelfs lichaamsdelen.

Shape_Form_Forme_Vorm

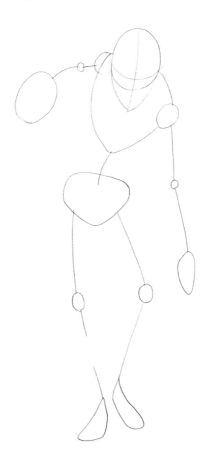

All the extremities are bent in some way.

Alle Gliedmaßen sind mit Bandagen umwickelt.

Toutes les extrémités sont courbées d'une façon ou d'une autre.

Alle ledemeten zijn op de een of andere manier gebogen.

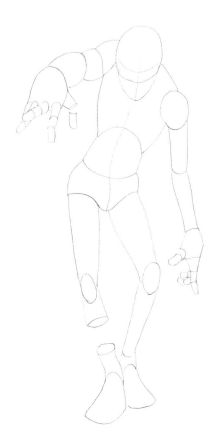

Draw the body in perspective. The inclination of the hips also affects the shoulders. Do not draw any of the calf.

Gib der Gestalt Perspektive und achte auf die Neigung der Hüfte und der Schulter. An einer der Waden sind die Knochen sichtbar.

Dessinez le corps en perspective. L'inclinaison des hanches affecte également les épaules. Ne dessinez rien du mollet.

Teken het lichaam in perspectief. De schuine houding van de heupen is ook van invloed op de schouders. Teken geen kuiten.

Anatomy_Anatomie_Anatomie_Anatomie

The body is covered in wrinkles, bits of skin, dry patches and stains. A tear in the leg leaves the tibia and fibula visible.

Der Körper ist von faltigem, zerfetztem Stoff umgeben und mit Flecken übersät, an einem der Beine sind Schienbein und Wadenknochen freigelegt.

Le corps est couvert de lambeaux, de bouts de peau, de bandes sèches et de taches. Une déchirure à la jambe laisse voir le tibia et le péroné.

Het lichaam zit onder de rimpels, stukjes huid, droge plekken en vlekken. Eén been is gescheurd zodat het dij- en kuitbeen zichtbaar zijn.

Cover the mummy with an old-looking bandage, respecting the volume of the figure.

Bedecke die Mumie mit alten, abgewetzten Bandagen und beachte dabei die Körperhaltung.

Couvrez la momie de bandelettes usagées, en respectant le volume de la figure.

Wikkel de mummie in verband dat er oud uitziet; houd daarbij het volume van de figuur in de gaten.

Lighting_Licht_Éclairage_Licht

Do not use flat shadows. Adapt them to the volume of the body, as the bandages create small protrusions.

Verwende keine flachen Schatten, sondern passe sie dem Körper an. Auch die Bandagen werfen kleine Schatten.

N'utilisez pas les ombres plates. Adaptez-les au volume du corps, tandis que les bandages forment de petites protubérances.

Gebruik geen vlakke schaduwen, maar pas ze aan het volume van het lichaam en het ongelijkmatige oppervlak van de windsels aan.

Separate planes by reinforcing the intensity of the shadows and colors in the foreground and toning down those in the background.

Grenze die Bildebenen voneinander ab, indem du die Schatten und Farben im Vordergrund verstärkst und den Hintergrund dezenter gestaltest.

Séparez les plans en renforçant l'intensité des ombres et des couleurs au premier plan, et en atténuant celles de l'arrière-plan.

Grens de vlakken af door de intensiteit van de schaduwen en kleuren op de voorgrond te versterken en die op de achtergrond af te zwakken.